Keeping The Fire

Sustaining Revival Through Love: The Five Core Values of Iris Global

ROLLAND BAKER

RIVER
PUBLISHING

River Publishing & Media Ltd
Barham Court
Teston
Maidstone
Kent
ME18 5BZ
United Kingdom

info@river-publishing.co.uk

ISBN 978-1-908393-55-5

Contents

Foreword

For thirty-five years I have walked together with my beloved Rolland among the fields white for harvest. Together we have passionately loved Jesus! Together we have learned from and loved the poor. Together we have pursued with every fiber of our beings our God who is worthy of it all. Together we have raised our beautiful children who teach us what love looks like. Together we have fellowshipped in His sufferings and experienced more of His glory than we ever dreamed we would.

We believe for a huge tribe of lovers of God to burn with His holy fire and go to the darkest places on the planet. As you read *Keeping the Fire*, you too will be set ablaze!

Heidi Baker
Mozambique
October 2015

Preface

by Elisha Baker

This is a work about lineage.

At first glance it might appear to be concerned with a lineage of flesh and blood, but that is not the one I am concerned with here. Families often do pass on a spiritual lineage, because children are often (though assuredly not always) in an excellent position to stand upon the heights their natural parents have captured for them. Such a lineage exists in and belongs to those with the will and the grace to take hold of it. It is for those who honor spiritual fathers to be spiritual sons.

Several years ago my father nearly died of cerebral malaria. When I visited Mozambique last summer – as I have done every summer since I moved to America – I was told I should tell him goodbye.

Technically, I suppose this was a unique experience. But for me it was not an unusual one. My mother and father have been imprisoned, mugged, deported, robbed, and assaulted by more diseases of the developing world than we have means to diagnose. They receive more death threats than we bother to count. They have been beaten with varying severity, and stood many times at knife-point or gun muzzle. They have often faced armed extortion, angry mobs, burglaries, fraudulent blackmail, car-jackings and street muggings. I have heard dire warnings from many doctors about their imminent demise. My mother, in particular, has recovered from more than one diagnosis of some incurable disease (and for all the miracles we have seen, I still hope each one is the last).

They have faced riots, some personally directed at them; the latter having arisen because desperate people wanted more from them than they had to give. They have faced accusations from spying for the CIA to drug trafficking to selling the organs of orphans on the black market (providing children's brains to the witch doctors for potions, as one rumor had it—for which a furious crowd once chased one of our staff members through a cluttered marketplace in Maputo). My mother has never been shipwrecked, quite, but last year she came very close during bad weather off the coast of northern Mozambique. Her boat was swamped, and she was given a ride home by a canoe full of naked fishermen. One of the men swam to shore and back to fetch them all clothes, so that she would not be uncomfortable while they rowed her back to civilization.

My family has taught, by the entirety of their lives, these words: *"He who seeks his life shall lose it, but he who loses his life shall find it."* All of my youth's instruction has been that it is worth any price to serve the Lord. Constantly to offer your life for His sake, and for the sake of those He loves – even for the sake of those who are yet His enemies – is the only kind of life that is worth living. This is the truth.

You are born for union with God. In a way that is uniquely proper to you, you are to act as God towards the world, and as the very Almighty toward all who are in it. The danger of doing this is exquisitely real. It is also inseparable from its glory. You are to be glorious. To live out this union risks pain for you, your loved ones, and all who love you. For Jesus it led to torture and death – and ultimately to the similar deaths of most of His disciples. If you are like Jesus, your pains will come through no error of your own. If, however, your mind is not yet entirely conformed to the likeness of His (and who claims it?), some of your pains will also come from your errors.

It is nonetheless worth risking the possibility of errors, and the greater errors that descend from greater dreams. It is worth daring to act like God. It is worth stepping out of a boat in the belief that you can walk on water. It is worth going to the ends of the earth. If need be, it is also worth staying in a place that may kill you. It is, my word on it, absolutely worth putting even your children in a certain kind of danger. In this world you cannot keep them from danger. But your absolute obedience to God will be to them the greatest inheritance imaginable. It is mighty lineage.

Do this, and they will indeed have to choose for themselves how to respond to the trials you will have subjected them to. Whether in response to your successes or your failures, they may make foolish choices. They may hurt. They may fail. They may learn things that you did not. They may fall short. They may surpass you. They may do both, in different times and ways. But in this way and in this way only you will have literally given them the best that any parent can give. If they wish to take them up, then at their hands will lay immortal riches, refined by fire. These are worth the cost, for our Lord did not lie:

"No one who has left home or brothers or sisters or mother or father or children or fields for me and the gospel will fail to receive a hundred times as much in this present age (homes, brothers, sisters, mothers, children and fields—and with them, persecutions) and in the age to come, eternal life."

If you walk hand-in-hand with your loved ones through the valley of the shadow of death, fear no evil. I say He makes no promise that you will never have to lay your firstborn upon an altar. My great-grandfather did, in a manner of speaking. But God loves your children more than you. And lineage – lineage! Leave this lineage to them in its purity, and you will yet see a great mystery, as great as the sacrifice of God's own child.

By that mystery, in all the heavens it will surely be said of your children – as many as desire that which you have left for them – He will cover them with his feathers, and under his wings they will find refuge; His faithfulness will be their shield and rampart. They will not fear the terror of night, nor the arrow that flies by day, nor the pestilence that stalks in the darkness, nor the plague that destroys at midday. A thousand may fall at their side, ten thousand at their right hand, but it will not come near them. "Because they love me," the Lord will say, "I will rescue them. I will protect them, for they acknowledge my name. They will call upon me, and I will answer them. I will be with them in trouble. I will deliver them. I will honor them. With long life I will satisfy them, and show them my salvation."

Elisha James Baker

Chapter 1

Prologue

There has been much talk in recent years of revival. So much so that it makes me wonder at times whether revival itself has become the object of devotion.

I want to begin by saying that historically and biblically, the focus and subject of revival is not the work of the Holy Spirit or the dramatic increase in numbers in the churches that are affected by the breath of God. It is Jesus Christ, born of a virgin, who suffered under Pontius Pilate, was crucified, buried, resurrected, ascended and glorified.

Revival is about the Reviver,
nothing more and nothing less.

When the Holy Spirit falls upon a community, a city or even a country, many people discover a new affection for the person of Jesus. They bow down under the weight of the glory of God and worship Jesus, exalting Him for His supremacy and His primacy over all others. They fall in love with Him all over again and nothing can eclipse this love.

The Apostle Paul once wrote:

"I am afraid, lest as the serpent deceived Eve by his craftiness, your minds should be led astray from the simplicity and purity of devotion to Christ" (2 Corinthians 11:3 NASB).

When revival falls, people fall in love with the Reviver. They rediscover what Paul talks about here: *"the simplicity and purity of devotion to Christ."*

In June 2010, after over three decades of living in revival in Mozambique, I wrote about the importance of alignment – of staying on the central path of a simple and pure adoration of Christ, especially when other subjects are clamoring for our attention in the Church:

"We stay on track through all the differing ideas and streams in the Church by maintaining our simplicity and purity. We fix our eyes on Jesus, the author and perfecter of our faith. When pressed to the absolute limit, as was Paul, we determine to know nothing but Jesus and Him crucified — the only basis of our confidence. He is the dividing line, the stumbling block, the cutting edge, the point at which we meet salvation and life. No one in the universe is more controversial.

We trust and love Him because He died for us and rose again on our behalf. He is the one who suffered for us. He paid the penalty for our sins. He purchased our lives with His blood. He showed us what love is. And so we are loyal to Him alone. We belong to Him, and not ourselves. We make it our ambition to please Him. If necessary, like Paul, we will suffer the loss of all things in order to have Him. We forsake every temptation in this life that takes us away from Him, even slightly. He is our greatest pleasure, our ultimate companion. We no longer love the world or anything in it, because He is the supreme object of our desire. Worthy is the Lamb!"

Let me say right at the beginning that while I may mention revival a great deal in this book, my focus is on Jesus, not revival. I worship the Reviver, not revival, and certainly not the revived.

Similarly, while I talk a lot about missions, my devotion is not to a process or method of making disciples of all nations, but to the subject of the Gospel, Jesus Christ. Mission is first and foremost about Jesus. When a person falls in love, they cannot stop themselves talking with great passion about the subject of their affections. So it is with missions. I quote again from June 2010:

"It is impossible to be devoted to Jesus and not share Him, pure and simple. We cannot see Him now, but God has ordained that we love Him by loving each other, whom we can see. He is love, and so we cannot separate the first commandment from the second. There are many callings, but none higher than to give water to the thirsty and food to the hungry. The intercessors at home and the troops in the trenches are equals in the Kingdom. We learn to love just as we are gifted and called by God...

To us missions is the natural outworking of our faith. It is the way we return the love God has for us. There is no other option. Revival without missions is deficient. To turn away from the lost, poor and needy is to turn away from God. Our intimacy with Jesus extends to one another; such is the excellence and perfection of His Kingdom!"

Be in no doubt. This book is not a celebration of revival, of missions, or of Iris Global. It is not an attempt to unearth a key to church growth and explosive evangelism. Rather, it is a celebration of who Jesus is and what He has done. It is truly all about Jesus. As the Apostle Paul put it, *"Let the one who boasts boast in the Lord"* (2 Corinthians 10:17 NIV).

This book is about sustaining revival over decades. By that I mean it is a book about falling in love and staying in love with the person of Jesus Christ.

My prayer is that you will fall in love with Him with all your heart as you read these pages, and that you will not be able to resist giving that love away, wherever you place your feet.

Introduction

This book is about the five core values that have been foundational for living in sustained revival in Iris Global for three-and-a-half decades. These values undergird everything we are and do. Simply, they are:

1. Find God
2. Depend on Miracles
3. Go to the Least
4. Suffer for Him if Necessary
5. Rejoice in the Lord

These core values were mostly taken for granted in our early years. They seemed obvious from Scripture and we didn't see the need to highlight them in any special way. Of course we needed to find God and depend on Him, be humble, go to the poor, suffer for Him and rejoice in Him. This seemed self-evident. But over time we found, through more and more exposure to the many worlds of ministry around us, just how controversial these values are. Three-and-a-half decades later, even though they are extraordinarily definitive of our ministry, we believe they are thoroughly normative for the Church worldwide and for every Christian. They are part and parcel of the normal Christian life.

Our experience has only increasingly confirmed the absolute need for each of these five values. Iris Ministries would collapse with the loss of any one of them. We do not impose them on our ministry; the Spirit of God has imposed them on us. We simply recognize them and adopt them, both by choice and sheer necessity, and we continually perceive in hindsight how they have operated in our lives.

For example, we could not have designed revival in Mozambique. Revival is not something that we orchestrated. It was quite simply ordained and initiated by God. We can say it was triggered by spiritual hunger, yes, but that hunger was itself produced by divinely superintended preparation and this preparation came in the form of a great humbling of the entire nation.

Mozambique suffered five hundred years of colonialism and slavery. Over thirty years of warfare reduced its infrastructure to a shambles. From being the destination of choice for the adventurous rich of Europe, it descended to being the poorest nation on earth under communism and atheism. It was humiliated to the extreme, desperately dependent on foreign aid. Then in 2000 it was subjected to the worst flooding in recorded history since Noah, enduring torrential rain for forty days and forty nights. More damage was done by that flooding than all the years of warfare.

Severe droughts, AIDS, the world's worst medical infrastructure and educational system all contributed to bringing Mozambique to its knees before God. It had no national pride, no hope and no plan. It was in this atmosphere that we saw a massive cry for God rise up all across the country – one that we had never witnessed or heard of either in all our combined experience, or in our studies of church history.

That cry was initiated by God not by human beings.

Heidi and I alone could do nothing against such a challenge. We were not backed by any church. No one sent us or supported us at first. We had no strategy, other than to show up and trust Jesus. We stood alone on the streets of Maputo, thrilled at the chance to see what only God could do. He opened doors. He softened officials' hearts. He convicted victimized street children of their sin. He filled them with His Spirit and revealed Himself to them. He filled them with massive love, peace and joy. He motivated them to preach boldly and authoritatively on the streets. He began healing the sick and restoring hearts.

We had no intention of starting churches and building Bible schools, but extreme hunger among pastors demanded that we do so. Then He began raising the dead through our pastors and desire for God spread like wildfire through the bush and eventually through all ten provinces. No one could have stopped these pastors who could not help but leap from one village to another, starting churches in every village with no one telling them to do so. Signs and wonders exploded like bombs all across the country. People suffered extreme danger and hardship to come to our bush conferences because they heard "Jesus was in town." We had no money for beautiful facilities and impressive productions and we could never have triggered such fiery desire, but the Holy Spirit drew the people with power like we had never seen.

None of this began with a human program or some carefully constructed five-year plan. We always began with finding God and seeking the face of Jesus in everything (our first core value). We could not have lasted a single day without our second core value, depending on God's miraculous provision for every material and spiritual need.

We never could have earned the amazing favor we now have with the government without first going to the poor and not trying to impress anyone (our third core value). We suffered endless, repeated, impossible hardships and persecution, but did not retreat and protest (our fourth core value). This is the reason we are still serving in Mozambique.

We are criticized severely for rejoicing so extravagantly in the Lord (our fifth core value). People call us frivolous for being so joyful. But we challenge anyone to go through what we have gone through without a massive, continuous, daily dose of the joy of the Lord! It is our motivation, our reward and our greatest weapon, expressing all the faith we have in Jesus! And it is a gift straight from heaven.

Our five core values have been absolutely foundational for us, at the very least with regard to living in sustained revival for approaching four decades, which means living in a sustained, simple and pure devotion to the person of Jesus.

It may be helpful to give a brief summary of each before examining them in more detail.

What Makes Iris "Iris"

In September of 2010 we convened our key Iris leaders from bases around the world to pray, soak, worship, dream and find unity together. This was the first time we had done this and well over one hundred missionaries and nationals from dozens of countries descended on little Pemba in our remote corner of Africa. It was a truly memorable opportunity for clarifying why we do what we do.

For days we ate and drank, wept, laughed and celebrated together as we built each other up with faith-building encouragement and testimonies. We were awed as we began to grasp the extent of what God has been doing among us and the strength of our family bonding.

The meetings were also a chance for us as leaders to articulate as never before what it is that makes Iris "Iris." The word "Iris" is Greek and also Portuguese for "rainbow". Heidi and I had begun as a Christian dance-drama ministry called "Rainbow Productions". We saw our different creative talents as colors of a rainbow that the "Son" shines through, giving a beautiful result.

Iris Global shares many values and points of doctrine with the wider Body of Christ, but Heidi and I have discovered that some key elements of our lives and ministry in Jesus are absolutely necessary, even if they are sometimes deemed by others to be controversial. We think they should all be normal in the Christian life and in Christian ministries everywhere, not special and unusual. However, we came to realize that in many parts of the Church they are far from normative.

Heidi and I began naïvely in these areas, but now realize we must prize, protect and nurture these values in our hearts and impart them to others. If we lose any one of these values, Iris would not function and be what it is today. When they all come together, it is as though we have a spiritual chain reaction, generating life and heat in the Spirit!

The following five values are not the only critical ones to us, but the Holy Spirit brought them to the forefront of our minds at our leadership meetings in Pemba in September of 2010. They are the building blocks for sustained revival.

1. Find God

We understand that we can find God and can experience intimacy, communication and companionship with Him in His presence if we share His love for righteousness. Mission has often been taught by others as unromantic; as disciplined obedience to the Great Commission. They teach that prayer is hard work, feelings are irrelevant, and getting the job done is what counts. They at least imply that we don't need spiritual experience to proclaim the Gospel. We can't expect immediacy and intimacy to be normal. We can function without the manifest presence of God.

At Iris we feel the exact opposite. We've gone through enough fire and hardship to know that without actually finding God, in fulfillment of Jeremiah 29:13, we cannot do what we do.

We cannot love with supernatural, unstoppable love unless we first experience the love of the Father ourselves!

As the radiance and exact image of the invisible God, Jesus is a spiritual lover, our perfect and ultimate companion. Our first value is to know Him in a passionate relationship with a love that is stronger than death (Song of Songs 8:6). We major first of all not on mission strategy, methods, projects and fundraising, but encountering the love that a love-starved world needs and craves. This does not mean that we are attracted to mindless, impersonal mysticism – to "experience" without content or relationship. No, Jesus is our heart's desire. We relate to Him with both our minds and hearts; we engage with Him, and find life and joy in our interaction. When we find Him, we find and gain everything. Without Him, we can do nothing of real value.

Therefore we start by finding God and relying on Him!

2. Depend on Miracles

If pride is an attitude that says, "I can live my life without depending on God," humility is the exact opposite. Humility acknowledges that it is not by human might or human strength, but by the Holy Spirit that anything worthwhile is built for God. Thus we are totally dependent on Him for everything and we expect miracles of all kinds to sustain us and confirm the gospel in our ministry.

When facing great human need with our human frailties,

we rapidly reach the limits of our resources, wisdom and love. We face overwhelming poverty, sickness, demonic attacks and every kind of evil. But with excitement and joy we aim beyond what we can imagine doing in our own strength.

We humble ourselves, depending completely
on God's miracle-working power
for one breakthrough after another.

Heidi and I began our life of missions with the dream of living out the Sermon on the Mount, taking Jesus at His word that we did not have to worry about tomorrow. We imagined addressing extreme human need by example, living without anxiety, free to bless, always with pure motives, looking to God alone for what our hearts and bodies needed.

We believe we experience miracles because we value them and ask for them, understanding that He will give them to us only if they will not take us further from Him. For His sake we will lose our lives daily, knowing that by His power we cannot lose, but will be sustained and become more than conquerors. The engine behind the growth of Iris in Mozambique has been a marriage of love and power; we do not have to choose between them, but can look forward to doing even greater works than Jesus while remaining in His love.

3. Go to the Least
We look for revival among the broken, humble and lowly,

and start at the bottom with ministry to the poor. God chooses the weak and despised things of the world to shame the proud, demonstrating His own strength and wisdom.

*God's ways are the reverse of the ways of the world.
At Iris we waste our time on those without influence,
stopping for the one.*

We will go anywhere, if possible, to minister to the meek and desperate, the poor in spirit, who truly understand their need of God. We will go to the neglected, the forgotten and the lonely.

Loneliness may be the most terrible scourge of the human spirit. Its love-starved emptiness threatens pain and terror as it advances, destroying all joy and hope in its path.

In Mozambique, the world's poorest country, loneliness strikes abandoned children in huge numbers and with wicked ferocity. We can choose to look away, or in Jesus we can open our hearts to see, feel and absorb the awful damage that Satan has done to so many. If we have it in our spirits to look for and rescue the lost and hurting, if we will not shield ourselves from an awareness of the overwhelming need, if we will intercede desperately and brokenly for children who are not even our own, we will participate in God's nature. We will share in his glory and future. We will see His salvation and deliverance. We will be part of his plan. We will be useful to Him, a pleasure to Him, an altogether worthy and romantic delight to His heart. By going to such as these, we participate in the mission of Jesus, who proclaimed Good News to the poor.

4. Suffer for Him if Necessary

Depending entirely on the miracle-working power of God does not mean that we seek only to see the glory of God and never expect to experience Christ's sufferings. We understand that a true son or daughter of God not only encounters supernatural signs and wonders, but also great hardship. Indeed, we understand the *value* of suffering in the Christian life. Learning to love requires a willingness to suffer for the sake of righteousness. Discipline and testing make saints out of us and produce in us the holiness without which we will not see His face and share His glory. With Paul we rejoice in our weaknesses, for when we are weak we are strong. Under great pressure we learn to rely on God, who raises the dead (2 Corinthians 1:9).

Jesus was rewarded for enduring evil opposition without sin. Our reward in heaven will be for the same. We resist sin to the point of shedding our blood, if necessary, by considering His example (Hebrews 12:3). Jesus is glorified now not because He exerted His power against His enemies, but because He overcame them with love. That kind of love entails suffering – the willingness to turn the other cheek, to go the second mile, to deny ourselves, to pick up our cross and follow Him. He showed us the only way to be counted worthy and the angels sing of him, "Worthy is the Lamb that was slain to receive power and riches and wisdom and might and honor and glory and blessing" (Revelation 5:12). There are no shortcuts here.

"Now if we are children, then we are heirs — heirs of God and co-heirs with Christ, if indeed we share in his sufferings in order that we may also share in his glory." (Romans 8:17)

So, as sons and daughters, we are prepared to embrace pain as well as power.

5. Rejoice in the Lord

Having said all that, the joy of the Lord is not optional and it far outweighs our sufferings! In Jesus it becomes our motivation, reward and spiritual weapon. In His Presence is fullness of joy and with Paul we testify that in all our troubles our joy knows no bounds (2 Corinthians 7:4). It is our strength and energy, without which we die.

The supernatural joy of the Lord may be the most controversial of our core values. But our aim is to impart so much of the Holy Spirit that people cannot stop bubbling over with love and joy! We pass through conviction and brokenness, even daily, but we are not left there. The Kingdom is righteousness, peace and joy in the Holy Spirit, in that order (Romans 14:17). And in His joy we are all the more capable of compassion for others, unfettered by our own sorrows.

Heidi and I could never have endured this long without a river of life and joy flowing out of our innermost beings. We are not cynical and downcast about the world and the Church, but thrilled with our perfect Savior, who is able to finish what He began in us. We gain nothing by being negative, but we overcome the world by believing that we can cast our cares on Him, thereby exchanging a heavy burden for a light one.

Joy, laughter and a light heart are not disrespectful
of God, nor are they incongruous in this world,
but are evidence of the life of heaven.

We are not referring to cheap and foolish levity that ends in grief, but exultation in the truth and reality of our salvation, a powerful work of the Spirit. We identify with the captives of Israel who were brought back to Zion filled with laughter and with songs of joy on their lips (Psalm 126).

No Guarantees

The extreme pressures and challenges of our ministry have led us to emphasize these five particular core values. They have enabled us to survive and continue to witness, against all odds, a revival that has far exceeded our expectations.

Now for a crucial question: *do these five values constitute a model for pursuing and experiencing revival? Put another way, if others embrace these five values, will it guarantee sustained revival in their lives and ministries?*

We are reluctant to say yes.

We don't believe for a moment that the ways of God can be reduced to a simple formula. The world, and increasingly the Church, runs after programs that offer four steps to success in your business, seven steps to effectiveness as a leader, ten steps to financial prosperity, twelve steps to freedom from addiction. We are not saying that these programs do not have any benefit. What we are saying is that the Holy Spirit is unlimited and therefore any attempt to create a program for understanding or experiencing Him is bound to be reductionist and simplistic. It would be like trying to bottle a tornado.

Experimentation in the field of quantum physics has demonstrated that no one scientific model is sufficient to apprehend reality. We need multiple models. If that is true of observed physical reality, how much more of God? No one side of an issue can contain or express God's ways. Most doctrinal wars are the result of insisting on only one model of perception. But it would be terrible if the truth were located on either one side or the other of most disputes. We must give God more credit, expand our minds and appreciate His perfection through the use of multiple models and perspectives.

All this is really another way of saying that we have no idea how to design a program that can be proven to consistently produce the kind of encounter with God that we have enjoyed and live for in Iris. The five values that we celebrate in this book have been foundational for both our identity (who we are) and our ministry (what we do). But they are not a five-step program for revival, nor are they a model for missions in every context. They are simply *our* core values.

An Incomplete List

The folly of turning our values into "five steps to revival", or "five keys to mission," can be seen in the one simple fact that there may, in any event, be more than five values undergirding our lives and ministries. In fact, we could probably add a sixth core value that specially marks Iris, and that is *freedom from control issues.* We want the Holy Spirit to be in complete control of us. Surrendering to the

Holy Spirit in all things, abandoning ourselves to the river of God in all our decisions and needs, is absolutely critical in Iris Ministries. We depend entirely on the Holy Spirit. He's the one in control, not us.

Yielding to the work and the ways of the Spirit is what enables us to see the power of God at work. When we rely on our own powers and strengths, we lock ourselves into a mentality that says human programs and natural resources are enough to change peoples' hearts and situations. But they are not. This is why, even when it comes to providing relief to those who are in need of food and medicine, we do not depend on our own plans or on worldly finances. We depend entirely on the power and the glory of God.

In other words, in our desperation we let the Holy Spirit control every part of the process.

This means that we have constantly been startled and amazed by the ways in which the Holy Spirit has provided heavenly answers to practical, earthly problems. We have seen time and again that the Holy Spirit is a Niagara Falls of grace; a cascading, thundering, refreshing, white purity, capable of carving through the hardest rock of human hearts, leaving eternal monuments to the glory of God.

If there is a sixth core value in Iris, it is letting the Holy Spirit have complete control of everything we are and do and watching as His ways trump and outdo ours in every respect every time.

Be advised, then, this is not an exhaustive and comprehensive list. There is more to God's ways among us than we can summarize in this book. His infinite wisdom is not reducible to finite words. As the early Church fathers knew all too well, a comprehended God is no God at all. As the Apostle Paul says in Ephesians 3:17-21 (The Message):

"I ask him [the Father] that with both feet planted firmly on love, you'll be able to take in with all followers of Jesus the extravagant dimensions of Christ's love. Reach out and experience the breadth! Test its length! Plumb the depths! Rise to the heights! Live full lives, full in the fullness of God.

God can do anything, you know—far more than you could ever imagine or guess or request in your wildest dreams! He does it not by pushing us around but by working within us, his Spirit deeply and gently within us.

Glory to God in the church!

Glory to God in the Messiah, in Jesus!

Glory down all the generations!

Glory through all millennia! Oh, yes!"

Chapter 1

Find God

"'In those days when you pray, I will listen. If you look for me wholeheartedly, you will find me. I will be found by you,' says the LORD."
(Jeremiah 29:12-14)

Three years after the first global team meeting I described in the introduction, our Iris leaders from over thirty nations met again at our base in Pemba, Mozambique. For three days in late July 2013 we united together as one intimate family to love, enjoy and encourage each other in the Lord. It was an extraordinary time of marveling at how God had enriched us with ever-increasing depth, fruit and numbers. We felt closer to each other than ever and more thrilled than ever before at the privilege we had of being a part of all that God was doing through us. Toward the end of the first meeting, I was spontaneously invited to share our five core values. I began with this prayer:

"Jesus, I pray that you will accomplish everything you brought everybody here for in these GTM meetings. Don't let anybody escape. Give them everything you brought them here to give them. I ask, Jesus, that you would give them more in these next few days than they ever dreamed possible. I ask for shocking, surprising, unexpected things! Fresh, new, special ... If you want a people, Lord, to serve you; if you want a people that will follow you, obey you, do anything you ask them to do; if you want instruments, if you want a body, if you want hands and feet and brains, here we are.

Here we are on the altar. We offer ourselves on the altar. We want to give you, Holy Spirit, complete freedom. I don't want to control the meeting. I don't want to have an agenda. We have no ambition here, Lord. I, for one, would really like to see what you can do, Jesus, when you have complete freedom. We just want to get out of the way, and see what only you can do. Iris has never been about what we can do ... only what you can do. So have your way, Jesus! Have your way! Amen."

After praying I spoke about our first value, *finding God.* Here is a transcript of some of what I said:

"Let's think about 'core values.' What is important to us? What are we here for? What is at the top of the list? What are we trying to do? What is it that we want? What do we really believe in? What lights our fire? What makes us happy? What is worth suffering for? What is worth giving our lives away for? What's worth getting up in the morning for? What is it that makes us tick? What makes us move?

One thing we could say is 'revival.' How many want revival? Something needs to happen if we all want revival. You couldn't be a Christian if you didn't want revival.

What does 'revival' really mean?

Most of us are interested but we're not really overpowered by the idea of revival. I can remember in the United States, years before we came here, sitting in public restaurants reading books on revival and sobbing my head off, right in the middle of public restaurants. I wanted revival so badly! There have been times I have thought that revival is the only thing we can live for. This is it. We have to have revival. There isn't anything else! But not everybody is that excited about revival. And there are all kinds of ideas about what it is.

A lot of people define revival as 'churches that get a lot bigger'. Others call revival 'huge offerings'. Others call it 'transformation'.

I've heard people get so excited at conferences because they've taken more money in an offering than they ever have before, in the history of that particular conference. For them, revival is about prosperity.

At other times it's a huge number of decision cards that gets people excited. You wouldn't want to be a missionary if you didn't want to see people saved and go to heaven. Do you realize that at least one hundred thousand people die every day in the world without the Lord? One hundred thousand people every day! There is a heaven, there is a hell, and this is extremely serious. It's infinitely serious. Revival is important because it leads to multiple salvations.

And then we have those who stress the idea of heaven coming to earth and countries being transformed. I would *love* Pemba to be 'heaven on earth'. I would love for the country to be transformed through a visitation of heaven. I would love for all of the cars to work. I would love for the electricity to be on twenty-four hours a day. I would love to turn the tap on at the base and have water come out. I'd like to have a university that teaches mathematics and physics. I would like every family, every hut in Africa to have a refrigerator. I would like flushing toilets on outreach. I'd like schools that teach something. I'd like some doctors in the hospitals. I'd like some medicine in the hospitals. Yes, I would really love to see Mozambique become prosperous and healthy. I would like to be able to grow anything! So yes, I would just like to see heaven on earth! Wouldn't you like that?

But let's talk a little bit about what heaven really is. For one thing, Jesus said the 'kingdom of God' is not some place you can point to; it's inside you. We're preaching the kingdom and His righteousness; it's inside you. You cannot see it; the best part is inside. Everybody can carry heaven inside.

Let's suppose we had transformation outwardly. There are all kinds of good things we can do. We can build things, organize things, fix things and teach things. Many organizations concentrate on exactly that. These things give us a measure of satisfaction, a measure of interest. We can work on feeding people. Helping people medically is rewarding. But in speaking to our Iris leadership, I want to say something here: I'm hungry for more than that!

I'm hungry for much, much more than outward, physical transformation. As great and as good as these things are, they are not enough for the human heart. They are not enough to be the focus of Iris, not enough to be the reason we sacrifice and labor to do all that we do. Our hearts are hungry for more than that. Our hearts are hungry for *somebody*. Our hearts are hungry to feel and to experience love, peace and joy. Our hearts need to be on fire for a reason! Our hearts long to be in love with a perfect *Person*. Our hearts long for a perfect love affair. Our hearts have deep, deep, *deep* desires. Our hearts long for something we cannot even express. Our hearts long for our God!

Revival to me means your desire for God gets so extreme, so red hot, so fiery, that He's all you want! That doesn't mean we get nothing in the end. That means we get everything at the end!

Paul says in Romans 8, *'If God did not spare his own son, but gave him up for us all, how will he not also, along with Him, give us all things?'*

Jesus is all you need and everything you need! Everything good you could ever desire is inside Him. How can we express that massive, ultimate need, and our desire to find Him and experience Him?

God is capable of making you far more alive and more excited than you could possibly imagine. I have known and seen examples of people that are so extremely filled they can hardly stand it. The Spirit of God can fill you with light. He can really fire you up! He's the One who gives you joy! He's the One who gives you peace! He's the One who gives love!

It's an appetite for Him that we need.

This is our number one core value. *We must find Him, know Him, have Him!* He must be our most valuable possession! Nothing else matters!

The reason why this first core value is controversial is that many people have given up finding God and experiencing Him. But what keeps us going is believing, knowing and being confident that every day, all the time, we can find Him more, experience Him more and be more full of His Spirit.

We want to do much more than build roads, buildings and schools. We just want Him. We want to be deeply, deeply, *deeply* in love with Him! We want to be thrilled by God Himself! Yes, we've done good things and built farms and schools ... but I want something perfect! I want revival. I want a movement here that focuses right on Jesus' face and nothing else! I want Iris to focus on Jesus' face and nothing else! We only have one hope, one direction, one purpose. Jesus is the one we're excited about; He's the one we relate to. It's my relationship with Him that means everything.

I want a relationship with Him! I want to be in love! I want to be alive! I want the life that is in Him! I want the joy that He has. I want the mind that He has. I don't just want verses in a Bible. I don't just want correct doctrine. I don't just want a library of books on theology. I want more than a big church. I want more than anointing. I want more than to knock people down and make them laugh. I want JESUS!"

Extreme Desire

Our first value at Iris has therefore always been an extreme desire for the person of Jesus Christ. I believe that where this profound level of intense hunger grips a group of people on a consistent basis, there they will see sustained revival. Where people fall more madly and deeply in love with Jesus Christ, not losing their first love but intensifying it more and more, there heaven will come to earth and lives will be changed.

All this is to say that revival is not something defined by external factors – by larger offerings and churches, for example. It is defined and indeed initiated by something internal, by an unusual hunger for God birthed within the human spirit. When my spirit is prompted by the Holy Spirit to call out for more of the Father's love, more of the Person of Jesus Christ, then the seeds for sustained revival are planted. If I then choose to guard the soil of my heart and water these seeds, something will subsequently expand on the inside of me that overflows from my heart and my mouth, causing me to knock on the doors of heaven and implore the Lord of glory to pour out more of His love, His power, His manifest presence, His kingdom. Whenever two or three gather with this level of desire, then all things are possible.

Revival is accordingly hunger-driven.

Genuine revival has always begun when a person or a group of people have come to the end of their tether or rope. They have come to the end of their own transient resources and discovered the beginning of God's eternal, unlimited resources. This process is one of self-emptying, self-death even, in which we relinquish control to God and surrender ourselves to His love and power. When that happens the Holy Spirit comes, filling the empty spaces of our hearts, baptizing or drenching us with the Father's extravagant love and miracle-working power.

In January 1996 a friend was praying for me and for the work Heidi and I were doing in Mozambique. She saw a vision of black storm clouds over the country, the hideous mark of unrelenting war, famine, disease and death. But then she saw an opening in the clouds overhead. Serene blue sky appeared through a widening circle and a shaft of light beamed down into Mozambique. The Father's hand appeared and, as He pointed His finger, a stream of angels began to descend into that poorest of poor nations.

We had been feeling a discouragement over Mozambique's situation very nearly too great to bear. But then, from out of God's great heart we felt sudden strength, an immediate resolve to resist the devil fiercely and undo his damage, and to offer our lives again as living sacrifices for the Lord's purposes. God's magnificent promises will not fail, and we will not faint and lose heart. Instead we will endure and live to marvel at what God has planned for our lives and for this African country. We rejoice in the Father's love and goodness, reveling continually in His care, and know that we do in fact have the power of heaven and the angels before us and behind us as we seek to do the Father's will.

To live in sustained revival is to come back time and again

to this place of extreme desire and radical hunger for God, understanding that our desperation is the foundation for His manifestation – and it is this manifestation which fills us with the divine love that alone brings transformation.

A Love Affair with God

The number one reason why we long for this is because when revival comes the Holy Spirit reignites our love for God and fills us with a fresh love for those whom we are called to serve. When the Holy Spirit visits our hearts, we fall in love with God all over again. This love then becomes the true, and indeed, only valid wellspring for effective mission. Without this love burning like an unstoppable fire in our souls, there would be no lasting transformation in Mozambique or anywhere else in the world. We must therefore consistently be baptized, saturated and immersed in the Father's love.

In light of this we have to learn to put the Great Commandment before the Great Commission. The Great Commandment is the Love Commandment. This is stressed in Mark 12:

"One of the teachers of religious law was standing there listening to the debate. He realized that Jesus had answered well, so he asked, 'Of all the commandments, which is the most important?'

Jesus replied, 'The most important commandment is this: "Listen, O Israel! The LORD our God is the one and only Lord. And you must love the Lord your God with all your heart, all your soul, all your mind, and all your strength." The

second is equally important: "Love your neighbor as your-
self." No other commandment is greater than these.'"

What could be clearer than this? The highest priority we
have is to fall in love and stay in love with God. This love
must captivate every part of our lives. It must arrest one's
heart, soul, mind and strength. It is not enough to have a
purely cognitive love for God. What kind of love would it
be if the mind alone was impressed? No, this love needs
to grip every part of us. Only when we are seized by this
affection at every level and in every part of our lives will
we be truly empowered to love others and indeed love
ourselves.

This, then, is the Great Commandment.

What, then, of the Great Commission?

In Matthew 28:18-20, Jesus describes to us what this is
in what amounts to a mission statement:

"Jesus came and told his disciples, 'I have been given all
authority in heaven and on earth. Therefore, go and make
disciples of all the nations, baptizing them in the name of
the Father and the Son and the Holy Spirit. Teach these
new disciples to obey all the commands I have given you.
And be sure of this: I am with you always, even to the end
of the age.'"

The Great Commission is God's Great Mission. It is His
strategy for all those who follow His Son. This strategy
involves going to every nation on the earth and making
disciples. Making disciples means apprenticing others

to become passionate followers of Jesus. In practice this means creating groups of people who have bid farewell to their old life of self-rule and have instead placed their lives under the loving rule of God. It means helping others to do what Jesus did and to live as Jesus lived. It means leading people into the presence of Jesus, which is heaven on earth.

At Iris we honor the Great Commandment. We do not teach people to engage in mission until they are passionate lovers of God. Jesus Christ is the Bridegroom and we are His Bride. Only when a deep love for Jesus burns within our hearts are we able to love others and love ourselves. Only when we are truly in love with God are we able to go to the nations and make disciples of Jesus. Everything starts with a love affair with God Himself. When we have learned to obey the Great Commandment, then we can fulfill the Great Commission.

Hungry Children

Do you see how this first value is so important? We need to throw ourselves at the feet of Jesus, lavishing Him with our love, wiping His feet with our desperate tears. We must abandon ourselves to Him, as surrendered God-lovers, trusting Him and relying on His love and power and not on human programs and strategies. In short, we must always seek after God.

Revival history is full of stories about children and young people leading the way in being hungry for God. Not long ago I wrote this about the children we serve:

"The children are pouring their hearts out to Him, knowing that He is their only hope. Two Sundays ago the Holy Spirit fell on the children in church, filling every single child, and every one began praying and worshiping in tongues. So did each of our visitors from the city and the surrounding villages. We may be ministering to unimportant, uneducated, lowly people, but Jesus came to them, and nothing more wonderful could happen. He showed them what He thought of them, that He loved them, and He revealed Himself to them. Holy Spirit, continue to come and blanket our children with your sweet, warm, comforting presence. Bring grace like sweet, spring rain.

It is the change in the hearts and spirits of the children themselves that is most gratifying. They have repented in tears. They pray and worship from the heart, often long after our meetings are dismissed. Many pray in tongues and have felt the Holy Spirit's touch. They know they need the Lord more than anything material, but they don't hesitate to cry out for food and provision as well. They are much closer to each other, the older children comforting and caring for the younger. They laugh and play energetically, and in the barren simplicity of their existence they exhibit joy. They have hope again and they know it is because Jesus has come to Chihango."

It is truly a beautiful thing when children go after God. Just as they are often hungry physically, so they are hungry spiritually. This hunger is not a sophisticated longing. It is simple and sincere because children are not distracted by mission strategies, theological subtleties or outreach methodologies. Their hearts are uncluttered, trusting, eager, and open. Thus in Matthew 18 we read:

"Jesus called a little child to him and put the child among them. Then he said, 'I tell you the truth, unless you turn from your sins and become like little children, you will never get into the Kingdom of Heaven. So anyone who becomes as humble as this little child is the greatest in the Kingdom of Heaven.'"

Pastors as Trailblazers

We have learned how important it is for pastors to be hungry for God's presence. Pastors are in many ways the point men and women of a church. Whatever they set their face to, those following set their faces to as well. So it is vital that pastors value seeking after and finding the presence of God. If they are hungry, others will be too.

We see this in the lives of two biblical leaders in Judah in the 6th century BC. Zerubbabel and Joshua became desperate for God to intervene in a difficult situation. They were trying to persuade the people – about 50,000 in number – to stop doing home improvements and to get back to work on building the Temple in Jerusalem. Nothing changed until the leaders were visited by two prophets, Haggai and Zechariah. When that happened, they had an encounter with the Holy Spirit. Then the people had an encounter too. Within four years, the new Temple had been built and even the cynics – many of whom had been responsible for the discouraging delay in restoring God's house – cried out, "It's beautiful!"

When Heidi and I were ministering in Malawi in 2000 I wrote this about the local pastors whom we were trying to instruct, encourage and mobilize for revival:

"Their response grows. And then on the last day the floodgates of heaven are opened. Heidi preaches from the book of James on the practical realities of holiness, trying to condense a training program for pastors into one session. New churches are forming almost every day and we must teach leaders quickly what they most need to know. Do they want the purity of God? Do they want to be washed by the blood? Do they want the power of the Holy Spirit? Do they want the wisdom of God to lead their people?

We pray for the pastors first. They throw themselves down before God, oblivious of heat, wind and blowing dirt. A mighty cry of prayer goes up to heaven. Young and old weep together. Rivers of tears flow. Hands reach toward God. Many are shaking in their intensity, unaware of anyone else but Him. Lost in worship and desire, many are pouring their hearts out in tongues.

We invite everyone to jump into the things of God, to come forward, join the pastors and seek Him. And then for hours our conference becomes something like a Day of Pentecost for Malawi. No one cares about time, appearance or comfort. Even children are hit with the fire of God. Waves of glory and gratitude roll over us all. The roar of prayer continues. Jesus is getting what He wants: extreme passion for Him!

This is what we came for, an outpouring of the Holy Spirit: visions, miracles, utter repentance and the richest love in the universe crashing down like a mighty, pounding cataract on the poor and abandoned of the world. Let the fresh, cool, refreshing mist of this living waterfall be felt all over Africa and the world. Let the brilliance of its perfection spread everywhere, with thundering power. Let the Holy Spirit roll like a tidal wave over the hopelessness of this entire continent, undoing Satan's worst.

The missionaries did come as promised, and so did the Holy Spirit. We have wildfire church growth in Mozambique, and now in Malawi too."

See how important it is for the pastors and leaders to lead the way when it comes to extreme passion for Jesus?

I Will be Found By You

Our experience simply serves to confirm what we see both in the Scriptures and throughout revival history:

The presence of God becomes powerfully manifest in places where there are people who are intensely hungry for Him and Him alone.

This has been our focus – seeking and finding God with all our hearts. It is foundational to who we are and what we do; the key to sustained revival.

As we have traveled throughout the globe, it has greatly blessed us to see people in many different countries and contexts becoming more and more desperate for the presence of God. Revival is a hunger-driven reality and wherever people seek after God with a Jeremiah 29:12-14 intensity, there revival fire is falling. As I wrote in March 2010:

"Heidi and I are back in Pemba after traveling since January on an intense ministry schedule that has taken us all over Asia, to Europe and across Africa. It has been a thrill to see the power of God fall on hungry believers all over the world. The Body of Christ is getting more and more desperate for God, willing to pay any price to experience His presence and companionship. There is no pleasure like walking and talking with Him, leaning on Him alone for every possible care and desire of our hearts.

How much more of Him do we want? He is able and willing to pour out His Spirit without measure. May we never lose our appetite for more righteousness, peace and joy in the Holy Spirit! All these are found only in our magnificent Savior, with all the intensity and fire of the author of life Himself!

This is not the time to be hindered by doubts, divisions and politics in the Church. We don't have room for worrying about titles, positions, credits and recognition. We can't be bothered with concerns over support and publicity. We don't know how to engineer and program revival. We are dependent on our God like humble little children. What we have already seen and heard has raised our expectations to new heights. He is able to keep us, and finish what He began in us. We can trust Him with our hearts, our spirits, our health, anything that has to do with our wellbeing.

His power among us knows no limits. He baptizes us with His Spirit, and all things are possible when that happens. Deep conviction and repentance, sobs of love and gratitude, tongues and prophecy, waves of heat, purest peace and refreshment, super hunger for the Word of God, visions and visitation, revelation, healing, floods of heavenly joy, insatiable longing, wrenching intercession, singing in the Spirit, angels all around, weakness under the tangible heavy weight of His Glory, a sense of wonder and awe at His presence...

We love His gifts, and all the touches and demonstrations of His love. They all propel us toward that ineffable goal written about by Christian mystics for centuries: union with God! *'The one who joins himself to the Lord is one spirit with Him.'* (1 Corinthians 6:17).

When fruits of character are joined by gifts of power, truly our lives reflect His glory and presence. We need His love in our hearts. We also need His anointing to accomplish anything. We need both Word and Spirit.

We are still learning to go lower still, which is the only way forward. And we are still learning to stop for the one in the middle of a sea of need. We are still learning what it means to be a friend of God, and to value fellowship with Him and each other above all else. We are not professional, high-powered, efficient missionary machines. We measure the quality of our lives by the depth of our relationships. We are learning to love."

Chapter 2

Depend on Miracles

"I came to you in weakness—timid and trembling. And my message and my preaching were very plain. Rather than using clever and persuasive speeches, I relied only on the power of the Holy Spirit. I did this so you would trust not in human wisdom but in the power of God."
(1 Corinthians 2:3-5)

I want to return to the gathering of Iris leaders from over thirty nations I mentioned in the last chapter. We met in Pemba, Mozambique at the end of July 2013. During those days I was asked to share our core values. This was not planned, so what came out of my mouth flowed from my heart.

In the last chapter I spoke about our first value, *find God*. Now I want to share some of what I said about our second value: *depend on miracles.*

Like Paul in 1 Corinthians 2:3-5, the message I imparted

was simple. The lower we go before the Lord, the more He will raise us up to minister in resurrection power, including signs and wonders.

Here are extracts of what I preached that night:

"When faced with such a perfect, glorious God, all we can do is go lower still. Bow before Him broken and contrite. Become nothing. There's no room for ambition in the kingdom of heaven.

People ask me, 'Pray for me, impart to me, I want gifts, I want power!' My first advice is to go lower. Become nothing at all, until your motives are pure, until there's no pressure on you. When there's no pressure, there's no competition.

It's so much fun to be nothing! It's so relaxing not to have to prove anything. It's so wonderful to see your brothers and everybody else doing better than you, being more anointed than you. It's fabulous to bless people for their success. It's great to be able to compliment people and lift them up. You don't even care where you are at the table – because you have a perfect Savior, you are set! If you have the number one core value, if you have Him, you don't have to worry about anything else!

God just loves the humble. He is opposed to the proud and gives grace to the humble. It's the only way to go. You want the key to the Christian life, want to please God, want to get more anointing? Just keep going lower, and lower, and when you've gotten as low as possible, go lower!

I have some friends who wanted to have a humility contest. Then Jesus showed up and said, 'Hey, if you're going to do that, can I play?'

Here's Jesus, the Lion of the tribe of Judah, the Alpha and the Omega, the Almighty God, and He's also the most humble person in the universe!

Spiritual pride and control issues are rampant throughout the Church. East, West, poor, rich – they are everywhere. We want Iris Global to be totally free of all these issues. Let's just have one big humility contest!

Pastors, you really need to honor one another, go lower still and not have a trace of ambition, except to please Him. God likes to demonstrate that Himself by going to the poor. At Iris Global we've always believed that the most likely place to find revival is among the poor, the humble, the nobodies, the ones with no influence.

For eighteen years Iris has now had influence and favor with many people. But if in the beginning we had tried to get that favor and influence, we would have never survived. If in 1995 we had tried to impress the government and tried to get pastors to follow us, we would not still be here. But we went to kids on the street whom the churches didn't want, the government didn't want. NOBODY wanted them. God loves to make something great out of nothing to prove His power and grace! He just loves to work with the humble and the nobodies. So, this is an Iris core value. We humble ourselves under the hand of our mighty God, and He exalts us at the proper time. We always go lower. Whenever there's a problem, the answer is to go lower."

What is Humility?

Many people misunderstand humility, but the simplest way of understanding it is by contrasting it with pride. Pride is not just a state of being, it is a state of mind. Before ever a person becomes proud in relation to position (state of being), they are proud in their hearts (state of mind). Pride therefore starts with an attitude.

So what is that attitude?

Pride is essentially the attitude endemic in the mind of unredeemed, fallen humanity. It is the attitude that says, "I don't need God to get by, to get on, to get up in the world. I can do these things in my own strength, with my own resources, in my own way."

At once we see how pride is rooted in sin. Sin is a three letter word with "I" in the center. Sin is at heart an attitude of mind that says, "I'm the center of my universe. I'm on the throne, not God. I'm in charge of my life. I'm in control. I call all the shots."

This attitude is basically a mindset in which fallen human beings repeat Adam and Eve's sin, seeking to take God's place. Pride is accordingly an attitude that seeks to elevate the self. It is Lucifer's original sin and Adam's. It is ours too when we say in our hearts, "Self will rule, not God."

Humility, on the other hand, is something totally opposite to this. The humble heart accepts its rightful place. I am a creature but God is Creator. I am the clay but God is the potter. I am very small but He is very great. I am the servant and He is the master.

When a person chooses to humble themselves before God, they choose to go very low before Him and say, "Apart from you I can do nothing. I depend on you completely. I trust in your implicitly. If I am to do anything significant for you, then it must be in your power and strength, not mine."

Trusting in God

I quote again from that night in Pemba. I was led by the Holy Spirit to stress the importance of relying totally on the power of God in all things. The man or woman who is humble, who goes low before Him, is the man or woman who relies completely on Him:

"Our second core value is that we depend on God for everything. And I do mean *everything*.

What do I do if I don't have enough love? I depend on Jesus for more!

What do I do if I don't understand what to do next? I depend on Jesus to help me understand.

What do I do if we don't have enough money? I don't write a newsletter, I depend on Jesus for more.

What if I'm not anointed enough for certain things? I ask Jesus and depend on Him to give me everything that's good. I don't trust in myself at all.

Paul says in the New Testament that we put no confidence in the flesh. We do not depend on ourselves for anything. We don't depend on the Body of Christ either. When we need something we don't just write a desperate letter to the Body of Christ and say, 'Please help us!' It's fantastic to trust in an all-powerful, all-perfect Savior.

God really is all-powerful and He can do anything He likes. He can change the hardest, meanest, most stubborn, murderous, most filthy sinner on the planet. Consider Saul. He was a Pharisee out to kill every Christian he could. And in three days God turned him into the first apostle, the first missionary, as an example for us all. I believe God can do that for anybody He wants!

Of course you ask, 'Why doesn't He do that for everybody? Why doesn't He treat everybody the same? How come some people get visions who have never even heard of the name of Jesus?'

I have made a choice and I believe this choice is from God. I just choose to trust Him! He knows more than I do! He's more powerful than I am! I'm the pot, He's the potter! Who am I to argue back to the Person who made me?

You can make your decisions, but you can't make good decisions unless the Holy Spirit is in you. We're not free to make beautiful, good, perfect decisions unless we're controlled by the Holy Spirit.

And so we trust God for absolutely everything at Iris Ministries. We trust God for people. We trust God for money. We trust God for timing. We trust God for healing. We trust God for materials. We trust God for everything!"

Going Lower and Lower

When the Apostle Paul went to Corinth, he made himself very low. He did not rely on mission methodologies. He did not depend on eloquent rhetorical arguments. He did not put his trust in impressive theological truths. No, he did two things. He first of all made a choice to proclaim the simple message of Christ crucified. In other words, he put his trust in the life-changing message of the Gospel, believing with all his heart that this simple message is the power of God for salvation. Secondly, he made a decision not to depend on the resources of his intellect or education. Rather, he relied completely on the power of God's Holy Spirit, so that when people and cities were transformed, those who marveled at this miracle would not elevate Paul but make Jesus famous.

This is the key to seeing hearts changed, sins forgiven, the poor fed, cancers healed, blind eyes opened and dead people raised. Only if we renounce our prideful inclination to rely on our own resources will we see heaven come to earth and people saved, healed and delivered. This has been something we have believed and tried to live right from the very beginning of Iris. We put huge value on going lower and lower before God, humbling ourselves before Him, trusting not in our own human strength and might, but throwing ourselves utterly and desperately upon God's resources to feed the hungry, heal the sick, raise the dead, receive financial breakthroughs … In short, to see the kingdom of heaven come on earth.

In September 2009 I wrote about how Heidi and I had recently been brought to a new level of total dependence on God's power in our extreme weakness:

"Heidi and I would both be dead by now if our doctors had been right.

A few years ago Heidi was in the hospital for a month with a staph infection that went out of control. The doctors gave up on her and told her she could write her tombstone! Then suddenly, while preaching in a lot of pain, God healed her, and the next morning she was out jogging!

Four months ago I was diagnosed with terminal dementia and was barely alive. I needed help to shower, change clothes, put on my shoes, clip my fingernails. I didn't know what country I was in, and couldn't remember anything from the day before. Heidi built a room for a full-time caregiver for me in Mozambique. Doctors said I wouldn't live long and family was called.

I had friends who wouldn't give up on me and they sent me to a Christian center in Germany where I received incredible medical care in a faith-filled environment. Today I am back in Pemba ministering the gospel, ready to fly my plane again, and reconnected with our friends and staff here. I look forward to pushing back the frontiers of missions in Sudan, the Democratic Republic of Congo and wherever the need is greatest.

We cannot function in this world without the power of our God. Some of us haven't yet been brought to our extremity, and so we aren't fully and forcibly aware of our dependence. But our time will come. We need Him to stay alive. We need Him for our health. We need Him for our healing. We need Him for righteousness, peace and joy in the Holy Spirit.

We need more than talk. We need more than church, a missions program or financial support. We need more than any human being can do for us. We need sheer, raw power in the goodness and love of God. We need power to appreciate our God, to make Him the greatest pleasure in our lives. We need power to rejoice with joy inexpressible and full of glory. We need power to experience His Kingdom, to move in His environment.

How do we get power? The answer is that it is the grace and gift of God. God Himself plants in us an intense hunger that will not be denied. He opens our eyes to our spiritual poverty without His powerful presence. He grants faith where there was none. In His power we can rest even while under demonic attack. His power fixes our eyes on Him. In His power we are able to discipline ourselves in everything. We can cast our cares on Him because He is willing to use His power on our behalf.

How can we be sure He cares for us? The cross. We go to the cross always to find confidence to approach Him. We will not empty the cross of its power. There and only there we find salvation of every kind. At the cross we come to know our God and His heart toward us. At the cross we learn to become utterly dependent on His power."

A Cross-Shaped Key

The key to the miracle-working power of God is shaped like a cross. This Cross-shaped key is what opens the door to signs and wonders in our own lives and in the lives of others. As we die to ourselves, as we die to sin – our determination to manage and succeed in our own strength – we put our flesh to death and go through our own process of self-death, taking up our cross daily in obedience to Jesus.

But this isn't the end of the story, any more than it was for Jesus. Jesus died but He rose again. He was in the tomb for two days, but on the third day God the Father sent the miracle-working and death-defeating power of the Holy Spirit from heaven. The grave-busting Spirit of God invaded that place of death and utterly and miraculously transformed a dead corpse into a living Lord!

When we go low before the Lord, submitting to the death process that flows from His heart of love, we position ourselves for mighty breakthroughs. We confess our weakness before the Father and He in turn pours out His life-giving power into us. When we go low and humble ourselves we therefore make space for our own lives to be filled with that same power that raised Jesus from the dead. After our own Good Fridays, we brace ourselves for Easter Days!

This is why in Iris we have never been able to collude with those who stress the work of the Spirit, but who neglect the work of the Cross. We believe that Abba Father wants to turn us day by day into sons and daughters who truly resemble His Son, Jesus. Jesus accepted suffering as well as glory, pain as well as power. We cannot be conformed to His image, which is the grand goal of authentic discipleship, without doing the same. As the Apostle Paul wrote in Romans 8:16-17:

"His Spirit joins with our spirit to affirm that we are God's children. And since we are his children, we are his heirs. In fact, together with Christ we are heirs of God's glory. But if we are to share his glory, we must also share his suffering."

In other words, just as Jesus chose to go low and embrace death, so adopted sons and daughters do the same.

Miracles in Africa

As we have gone low and depended in our weakness on the power of God, we have seen every kind of miracle.

For example, we have seen miracles of provision.

At one point a large, three-month supply of food destined

for Chihango simply disappeared, apparently stolen by officials. Our storeroom was literally down to four bottles of ketchup and some herb tea, and that was it! We did not have money ourselves to keep feeding so many children. Everyone prayed their hearts out and the next day a truck unexpectedly arrived loaded with food from the United Nations World Food Program. Soon after that friends at the US Embassy directed the attention of the Mozambique WFP director to our situation, and an agreement was made to supply us directly with adequate maize and basic staples to feed the children in renewable three-month allotments! This cut our expenditure for food down by one-third or so.

Then we have seen miracles of healing.

One day a man called Joel came into our office to tell us what Jesus did for him. Joel caught malaria, but in the night a tall, shining angel touched him and placed a Bible in his hands. He was healed immediately and went on to be full of love and gratitude to Jesus, always ready to testify.

In Malawi an old man with a large, terribly infected ulcer on his foot came for prayer. It looked ghastly, like gangrene or cancer. I thought amputation was the only natural answer. We returned later and his foot was covered over with smooth skin. He grinned and laughed as he showed me his foot, which he was walking on perfectly normally.

In Chimoio a blind man spontaneously received his sight as we worshiped. He had been seeing light, but it was all a blur, and suddenly he could see clearly. He immediately called out and jumped to the platform to testify, completely thrilled.

In Dondo a man was near death, suffering from a huge

parasite in his abdomen. The hospital could do nothing. He couldn't sleep for fear of not waking up. During a time of healing ministry he felt a movement in his body and his pain and condition were gone.

During that same conference a little girl paralyzed from the waist down for eight months was healed. Her mother fervently preached to the crowd as the girl walked normally all over the platform.

We have also seen resurrection miracles. For example, Jesus used Surpresa Sithole, one of our leading evangelists, to raise Shansha, a six-year-old girl, who was dead from malaria for over a day.

In 2002, I wrote about another resurrection miracle:

"Lino is intense. His eyes are wide and lit up, his hands are waving and gesturing. He turns and shifts excitedly. He can't be quieted. He knows what he's talking about. He speaks with authority and I am listening, taking down every detail. He has been raised from the dead, and I want to know all about it.

Pastor Lino Andrade is one of our more than one thousand pastors in Mozambique. His mud hut church is in the town of Gondola in the central province of Manica, not far from Chimoio where we have had major conferences. He has just begun a three-month Bible school term with us at our Zimpeto center in southern Mozambique.

Today he testified in church and now I am with him face-to-face, getting every bit of information I can. This morning he declared earnestly to all our children, staff and Bible school students that life after death is real, the supernatural world is real, angels are real, and the power of Jesus is real. He should know. He is one of about ten people in our churches who have been brought from death back to life by the Author of Life, and we want to tell everyone!

Lino is a widower, and he stays with his daughter in her little house in Gondola. Not long before coming down for Bible school, he got seriously sick. He couldn't eat or sleep. He was in great pain. Too poor for medical attention, he didn't know what was wrong. Over the course of a month he kept deteriorating until he died.

Instead of burying him, his daughter called for Pastor Joni, also in Gondola, who came with four other church leaders to pray. For three hours Lino's eyes were rolled back into his head, and his body began to smell of decay. But Jesus has used Joni to raise the dead before and Joni was determined.

Lino was released from his body and given a vision of what might be. He watched his own funeral procession and could see others lowering his casket into the ground. He watched them put flowers on his grave. Two bright angels with wings came to him.

He was shown things that have not yet been explained to him. But in the vision Lino refused to accept his own death. And then he heard God tell him that he was not going to heaven yet, but that he had many more years to live.

In his spirit he could hear Joni praying loudly and fervently.

After a few hours he returned to his body and awoke in bed, but was very weak and nauseous from his own smell. Satan did not get his way and Lino was not buried. Lino gradually got his strength back and his body normalized as everyone around looked after him. His church and all who knew him are incredibly encouraged.

Lino himself is now strong and bold, always eager to minister."

Finally, we have also seen deliverance miracles. In 2002, I recorded the following incident:

"The rain is loud and the people in the back standing in the mud can hardly hear our simple sound system. What can the Holy Spirit do here? Plenty! Right now He is cleansing the entire assembly of demonic oppression. Tears are running down faces and bodies are shaking. Hands are lifted high. A huge outcry is rising up to heaven.

I have just asked how many are being harassed and afflicted by demons and nearly everyone stood up. Mozambique is riddled with witchcraft and demonic power, and so many churchgoers are syncretistic, going to witchdoctors as well as God to try to meet their desperate needs. Every chance we get in our Bible schools and churches we urge the people to make a clean and total break from powers of darkness.

So now I have asked the people to confess anything and everything still wrong in their hearts so that they can be cleansed and protected from evil forces.

Suddenly the Holy Spirit came in force and I can't preach over the sound of repentant voices loudly crying for mercy and help.

I and our pastors lay hands on as many as we can reach.

We rebuke all evil power.

Finally a mood of great peace and relief settles on every one and we move gently into the rest of our service."

Truly we have seen all manner of miracles.

The 3-D Gospel

This is so important to us. The reason why we spend so much time going low before the Lord is because we know in our hearts that the Gospel doesn't only provide salvation spiritually, or justice and mercy socially. The Gospel is also a supernatural Gospel. It brings miraculous healing to peoples' bodies.

For too long those who have been trained in missions have been taught to rely on human programs and strategies, many of which have been born from an academic mindset that puts trust in man's resources more than God's. We do not despise these things; we choose to honor and value the miracle-working power of God.

When Jesus started to extend the kingdom of heaven on earth, He made it clear that the Gospel He was proclaiming was a saving Gospel, a social Gospel and a supernatural Gospel.

It was first of all a *saving Gospel*. Jesus proclaimed Good News to the poor. He brought a message of freedom to those who were weighed down by sin and oppression. He forgave sinners and extended the Father's mercy to those who were broken and contrite in spirit.

This is one reason why Jesus was such Good News. He brought salvation to those who were prepared to go low and admit that they were sinners.

Jesus' Gospel was and is also a *social Gospel*. He didn't just attend to the spiritual needs of the people He came to serve as the Son of Man. He attended to their social needs too. He brought those who were on the margins into the mainstream. He did this by honoring women, exalting children, loving lepers, welcoming prostitutes and being a friend of sinners. Jesus brought God's extended Jubilee into history, setting the slaves free and even giving rest to the land. His Gospel is therefore one in which justice, freedom and dignity is given to those without power, without a voice, without any honor. It is a social not just a saving Gospel.

It was and is also a *supernatural Gospel*. Jesus restored sight to the blind. He caused the deaf to leap like a deer. He cleansed the skin of the leprous and He gave new body parts to those who had lost limbs. He still does these things today! We have seen it with our own eyes.

All this goes to show that anyone who is intentional about doing God's mission the Jesus way cannot rely on their own resources. They must be taught to be humble, to go lower and lower, and to rely on heaven's solutions to earthly problems. They must be taught that weakness, as the Apostle Paul taught, is the fertile soil in which God's miracle-working power can be manifested. They must be shown that the Gospel of Jesus is three-dimensional and includes words (preaching the Gospel), works (good works among the poor) and wonders (supernatural miracles). As I wrote back in 2002,

"We didn't come to Africa just to feed some children and give out a few clothes. We came to bring the wretched and forgotten close to Him, in the worst of circumstances. And we came to see what He can do when He draws close to them in return. Everything changes. All things are possible."

They, and we, must be taught that the glory of God shines most brightly through the cracks in broken clay pots.

Keeping a Healthy Perspective

At the same time, we have learned that people need to be taught to rely on the miracle-working power of God in a healthy, biblical way. This means that we have learned to see from different perspectives at the same time.

On the one hand, we truly believe that miracles are important because they can make people more receptive to the truth of the Good News about Jesus.

In 2009 I wrote this:

"As we emerge from the children's house we are met with a surprise. Moslem leaders in their caps and gowns have come to the village from the nearby mosque which serves the Moslem community of the whole area. They heard about the deaf being healed the night before and they want prayer too!

They bring us extravagant offerings – a pair of doves and a rooster! They also are touched and healed as we pray in the name of Jesus. They grin and are so pleased.

We leave them with a solar Bible.

May the love of God continue to spread across this

province as more and more come to know the power of the Cross."""

In this instance, it was when deaf ears were opened that unbelieving hearts were opened too.

On the other hand, just because a person receives a miracle, this is no guarantee that they will fall in love with God and choose to become a follower of Jesus.

In 2002 I wrote:

"By now we have had about a dozen resurrections from the dead in our churches. These result in sudden church growth and huge encouragement, but we have learned that not everyone is impressed or radically changed."

Love and relationship with God are not produced automatically by miracles. We have noticed time after time that even those raised from the dead and healed of serious diseases do not necessarily respond well to the Gospel or stay fervent and faithful to the Lord. Only one out of ten lepers healed by Jesus came back to thank Him. This understanding leads us to concentrate in our preaching and teaching not solely on external signs and wonders, but always on relationship. Churches deteriorate, pastors fall away, people lose interest, revival declines and our movement dries up if all we emphasize are prosperity, healings, manifestations and external phenomena. In Iris "doing the stuff" is not the point. Jesus is always the point.

When the miraculous occurs, pastors and leaders

may become highly energized and motivated to preach passionately the power and love of Jesus to villages a hundred miles around. But we understand that the very people who experience these miracles may not themselves attain the relationship with God that we preach. And witnesses of miracles may still not believe, no matter how obvious the evidence. We are convinced that one reason God does not do more miracles is that they often get more attention than He does. And no matter how great physical miracles are, relationship with God is even greater.

All this means that while we go lower and lower, depending more and more on the miracle-working, supernatural power of God, we do not place power above love in our thinking.

Falling in love with Jesus is the main thing.

Going Low with the Poor

We are to *be humble*. This means getting low before the Lord, renouncing our self-reliance and self-sufficiency, abandoning ourselves to the unending resources of an All-Sufficient God.

But there is another dimension to this as well.

We not only go low before God, we go low before others. We do this by choosing not to seek favor with those who are influential or wealthy when we begin to cry out to God for revival in a city or a nation. We go first to those who have no voice and no food. We go to the poor, the destitute, the bruised, the sick, the widowed, the orphaned, the forgotten, the ostracized, the outcasts and the dying. We who behave as nobodies before God go to those who are regarded as nobodies by man.

Being humble therefore applies not only to the vertical dimension of our lives (our relationship with our Father in heaven); it also applies to the horizontal dimension (our relationship with the poor to whom we are called to proclaim Good News).

This leads us to our third value, the subject of the next chapter.

Chapter 3

Go to the Least

*"Then these righteous ones will reply, 'Lord, when did we ever see you hungry and feed you? Or thirsty and give you something to drink? Or a stranger and show you hospitality? Or naked and give you clothing? When did we ever see you sick or in prison and visit you?'
And the King will say, 'I tell you the truth, when you did it to one of the least of these my brothers and sisters, you were doing it to me!'"*
(Matthew 25:37-40)

Sustained revival involves embracing the core value of going to "the least of these". In other words, going to the poor. This is our third value and like all our values it cannot be simply acknowledged intellectually; it has to be lived out from the heart.

At Iris we have always believed that effective mission consists of more than just preaching Good News. We have also believed it should involve going to the poor, the hungry, the orphan, the widow, the prisoner. We do not therefore believe that what is sometimes referred to as the Social Gospel (Jesus' mission to bring justice to those who have been denied it) should be separated from the Saving Gospel, or for that matter from the Supernatural Gospel.

We believe that the kingdom of God is holistic.

This means that we don't just preach heaven, but we prove the love of God by drilling wells, building simple churches and schools, supplying teachers, providing for orphans and abandoned women – doing whatever we can with what we have. At Iris, one of our five core values is to go to the poor and bring the love of God to those who have nothing, and to do this in practical ways.

In this way we adorn the Gospel with love and good works that people can enjoy and appreciate here and now. We revel in the transformation we can achieve in the Lord that gives the poor more of a taste of heaven. We love material blessings that come from the good hand of the Father. We love to feed the hungry, set the lonely in families, teach the unlearned and bring hope and a future to the destitute.

In all of this we do not seek to do good works simply for their own sakes. We do them because our highest goal is to point desperate people to Jesus. He is our salvation, our prize, our reward, our inheritance, our destination, our motivation, our joy, wisdom and sanctification – and absolutely everything else we need, now and forever. All His grace and power flow to us through the Cross and no other way. We say with the Psalmist,

"Whom have I in heaven but you? And earth has nothing

I desire besides you" (Psalm 73:25).

We are glad to be known as social workers and humanitarians and to have a reputation for doing good works. But all is in vain if we do not bring people to faith in our God and Savior Jesus Christ. We want to be known by His Name, first and foremost. Everything we do is because His compassion burns within our hearts and because we long to make Him famous throughout the earth.

Helping those in Need

Jesus taught us not to pass by on the other side of the road when we see someone in need. At Iris we have sought to embrace our third value, go to the least of these, ever since the beginning. Right from the start we have tried to live this out. It has never been enough simply to give intellectual assent to this value. It has had to be lived.

As early as 1995 I wrote this simple report of something Heidi did:

"Recently Heidi found a girl called Beatrice lying along the roadside, covered with terrible infected sores from head to toe. She was wearing only a rag with a string for underwear. Heidi got her to the hospital and the staff said it would take four days just to get the infections down enough to diagnose her problem. But now the girl is much better and is going to make it. We are sure she would have died shortly if she had been left to herself. Today she is smiling."

Notice a number of things about this incident.

First of all, Heidi did not preach to this girl. She gave a

helping hand. Secondly, the climax to the story is not a healing miracle. It is that the girl got help and got better. Thirdly, the lesson is this: going to the least of these is sometimes just a matter of stopping and helping. This is enough to bring heaven to earth in a person's life. It is enough to point a person to Jesus and to make them smile.

Sometimes it is not just an individual but an institution that God has called us to help.

In the same year of 1995, Heidi and I were alerted to the existence of a financially strapped children's institution desperately in need of a foreign sponsor. It was founded during the Portuguese colonial days, many decades before, as a correctional institution for delinquent minors. Its facilities were thoughtfully and efficiently designed: it had a slaughterhouse, bakery, machine shop, pigsty, chicken coop, wells and water towers, administration buildings, classrooms, dormitories, and even a small medical clinic — fifty-four structures in all.

This promising facility was spread out across a large, breezy, beautiful piece of land right along the ocean about six miles north of the capital city of Maputo. About a square mile, or 640 acres, it had plenty of room for further development. Its shortened Portuguese name was "Chihango".

Almost twenty years of civil war and socialism reduced the property's facilities almost to ruins. The government had no money to maintain anything. Marauding, drunken gangs had long since stolen everything of value, ripping out electrical hardware and plumbing and even tearing out door jambs and windows for firewood. Phone lines were

torn down and taken away in the night for their copper.
Plumbing was broken down. Sewage lines and septic tanks
had been clogged and overflowing for years. Weeds and
dust covered nearly everything. Windows were broken.
Worse, there had been almost no food supply. The children's
recent store of maize, given by a donor some time ago, had
given out and now each day they were down to a handful
of rice and a bit of tea in the morning.

Early in 1995 Heidi and I submitted a proposal to
the Mozambican government offering to develop the
property for humanitarian and spiritual purposes under
Iris Ministries. Only twice in the previous ten years had
there been any other offers of help but none had come
to anything. The government doubted our viability and
resolve as well; they stalled for months before giving a
response. Eventually a group of officials gathered together
and verbally agreed in principle to allow us the full and free
use of the land for the purposes outlined in our proposal.

We immediately began to visit Chihango to minister to
the children. We didn't have much of anything to offer
materially, but we started daily meetings.

A few months before, these children knew nothing of
God. They had never had anything really good happen
to them. Now they were all touched by the Spirit and
confessed their faith in Jesus. Each day they eagerly
awaited our truck and its load of workers. If we were late,
they waited patiently. They all ran to the meetings.

The children learned to believe in Jesus and love and worship Him. They laughed and sang songs of praise throughout the day. They were hungry for prayer. They called out

to God with tears. One day they followed Heidi all around the property on a "prayer march", laying hands on every building and anointing everything with oil, declaring God's promises and leaning on God for an abundant, steady flow of provision. Heidi preached her heart out to them, telling them that they could not wait for Westerners. God would use *them* to repair Chihango. God would raise them up spiritually and they would be a rich blessing to their country, provided they repented and stopped their lying, stealing and fighting.

The Holy Spirit began to move on the children more each day. Even staff members, previously attached to the property by the country's communist system, began to change their attitudes and their ways. Spontaneously they started cleaning up their rooms, washing feces off the floors and began to paint their walls. They wanted to study again in school and some even began to insist on an immediate Bible school at Chihango.

A year before there had been 80 children. Pretty soon there were almost 180. The government wanted to continue sending us problem children whom no one else wanted and we decided to take them if at all possible. Most of them were either orphans or abandoned by parents unable to care for them. Heidi started picking them up, one by one.

For us at Iris, living out the third value, going to the least of these, has meant lending a helping hand to individuals and to institutions.

Hugging Orphans

It has also meant bringing the Father's love to the fatherless, to the orphan. This is who God is, a Father to the fatherless and a Defender of the cause of the widow, who causes even prisoners to sing with shouts of joy (Psalm 68:5-6).

Here are some examples.

One day Heidi picked up a little boy who had just been abandoned along the roadside by his parents who lived 120 miles away. He hadn't eaten in a long time. Heidi prayed and wept with him, fed him and brought him to Chihango. Even though he was emotionally numb, every day he received more and more of the love of Jesus.

Then there was Constance, a little girl at Chihango who had been abandoned in the back of one of the buildings when she was only two. She began to allow Heidi to hold her in her arms, hug her and put her to sleep. She always used to run away from everyone. From then on she followed Heidi everywhere and we started to pray that Jesus would fully heal Constance's heart and deliver her from her severely traumatic past.

In 1996, Heidi wrote:

"Last week my daughter Crystalyn and I were out buying bread, and in the street we came upon a motionless boy dressed in rags and covered with sores. We thought this precious child was dead. I walked over to him and laid my hands on his shoulder. He woke up and looked frightened. I gave him some bread and began to ask him his story.

Everista (the boy's name) could not talk very well. He had not spoken for a long time. He did not know how old he was. He had never been to school. He knew his parents were dead and he was alone and hungry. The other street children found him odd and had been kicking him around. His body bore the marks of years of abuse. His fingers were scarred from nervous chewing. He scurried along the ground more like an animal than a human being. I asked Everista if he wanted to come and live with us. I spoke of our large family at Chihango. His eyes brightened. I took him home and washed his wounds. Crystalyn happily gave him some clothes and things to play with. We hugged him, prayed for him, and let him know he was loved."

Living out our third value means that we are compelled to take the Father's love to orphans. It means hugging them and helping them. Often it means giving them a good education so that they have a chance to make a difference in the world. That's why I was thrilled in 2002 when I wrote this:

"We are very excited about our primary school for our orphaned and abandoned children. Jesus has given us very dedicated Mozambican teachers, and they have poured their energy and hearts into these most disadvantaged of students. Our facilities are so bare and basic and the government has in the past given us such a hard time. However, our fifth and seventh grade classes took national exams and ninety-five percent of our students passed, giving our school the highest score in the country. Average is seventy percent. Jesus loves to take 'the least of these' and bring them to the head!"

In 2009 we were again excited when we were invited to a pastor's hut for a thanksgiving dinner. Our hosts did the most special thing they could by serving up their one scrawny chicken that they had killed earlier.

The next day we woke up early, wet with perspiration as the rising sun heated our tents. After coffee and bread, and lots of fellowship, we gathered with the villagers to dedicate a new children's house. We had been instituting a system of church-based orphan care in as many villages as possible, asking each pastor to take care of a dozen orphans. We assembled in the house to pray with our orphans, who were not orphans any more, but fully adopted into the family of God and by the Body of Christ in the village. The pastor, his wife and the new children under their care were beaming. We put together a child sponsorship program that we prayed would miraculously support these children and thousands more like them all over Mozambique.

Revival in Prison

Let's return for a moment to Jesus' teaching in Matthew 25, the passage in which He mentions "the least of these":

"When the Son of Man comes in his glory, and all the angels with him, then he will sit upon his glorious throne.   All the nations   will be gathered in his presence, and he will separate the people as a shepherd separates the sheep from the goats.   He will place the sheep at his right hand and the goats at his left.

Then the King will say to those on his right, 'Come, you who are blessed by my Father, inherit the Kingdom prepared for you from the creation of the world. For I was hungry, and you fed me. I was thirsty, and you gave me a drink. I was a stranger, and you invited me into your home. I was naked, and you gave me clothing. I was sick, and you cared for me. I was in prison, and you visited me.'"

Notice the phrase, *"I was in prison and you visited me."* Hebrews 13:3 exhorts us to,

"Remember those in prison, as if you were there yourself. Remember also those being mistreated, as if you felt their pain in your own bodies."

Going to the poor, to the least of these, has also meant taking the love of God to people in prison. There are many stories I could tell of our outreaches to prisons, but one dating from 2011 shows the difference revival makes.

"We stopped at the government's local prison, where the Holy Spirit has been breaking out under the ministry of one of our trusted staff, a long-time Iris missionary and close friend, and Ezekiel, an ex-prisoner.

The prison interior was grim, dark and claustrophobic, as expected. A few prisoners were still locked in their dirty, miserable confines, but most gathered in a long, narrow hallway with high, out-of-reach windows for security.

On entry, though, we were greeted with shouts of praise, and then with one voice the whole prison reverberated with fervent worship.

We joined them, standing transfixed as all these

'dangerous offenders' sang their hearts out with joy, energy and enthusiasm to the King of Kings. Jesus was obviously now their real reason for living, the hope of their lives, the joy of their salvation.

Rarely have we ever seen such powerful evidence of a change of spirit. The prisoners shook our hands, hugged us, laughed and cheered as if they were having an absolutely great day, which they were! And they seemingly could not stop worshipping.

This is the road to transformation, the cutting edge of revival: the One who died and rose again on our behalf! He is the perfect personification of the love and power we all need, and only our faith in Him will overcome this world.

The atmosphere in that dark, horribly depressing place was extraordinary under the circumstances. In the same way, His presence in our most difficult times is all and everything we need. Our hope in Him is secure, our future safely protected and reserved for us. We may be in prisons of many kinds, but we have a Deliverer!"

Feeding the Hungry

Have you ever noticed how radical Jesus is when He teaches about hosting meals? Jesus often ministered to others through meals. Those invited were frequently the most broken in society in His day. He provided an open and welcoming meal table for the poor and the prostitute. As a friend of sinners, Jesus invited people who could never have invited Him back to dinner. They were simply not able to host meals.

Perhaps this is one reason why Jesus tells all those who

follow Him to be as radical as He was in hosting meals. He never preached what He didn't Himself practice. Listen to what Jesus says in Luke 14:12-14:

"'When you put on a luncheon or a banquet,' he said, 'don't invite your friends, brothers, relatives, and rich neighbors. For they will invite you back, and that will be your only reward. Instead, invite the poor, the crippled, the lame, and the blind. Then at the resurrection of the righteous, God will reward you for inviting those who could not repay you.'"

Here perhaps we begin to feel something of the cost of going "to the least of these".

On December 26th 2000 we gave a Christmas banquet at our Zimpeto center, and to us it was a foretaste of the King's great banquet given for us all on that Great Day. We called in beggars from the streets, the destitute from the dump, prostitutes from the brothels, drug addicts and gangsters, and they all sat down together with our children, missionaries and Mozambican staff. Cooks worked all day on our chicken dinner, something we have only two or three times a year. Heidi shopped for days in South Africa, getting dolls, marbles, balls, toy cars and stuffed animals to add to all that was sent to us from around the world. Volunteers wrapped presents for weeks. We gave donated pants and shirts to the dump children, and a week earlier we brought wraparound skirts to the prostitutes so they would have something to wear for Christmas with us.

All of us, almost two thousand, sang and danced before

the Lord. More came to Jesus, kneeling before the King who came, simple and poor, to identify with us.

We began with a beautiful wedding for a couple who hadn't been able to get married before because the groom's house was washed away in the flood. He is one of our pastors and has been living in the corner of a friend's grass hut, but now we've built him and his new bride a new reed house.

We are abounding in good fruit, such as prostitutes who have come to Jesus and who now want their children back from our house for abandoned and HIV babies.

One ex-prostitute married Zacharias, a young man Heidi found on the streets three years ago. Jesus changed Zacharias from a mean, violent street fighter into a radiant man of God who now pastors one of our downtown Maputo churches.

If we want to minister to the least of these, then it is vital that we feed the hungry and clothe the naked. The Word of God tells us that this is essential if we are to experience sustained revival. When we make this kind of emphasis a *lifestyle*, then salvations and healings happen quickly and God's glory is made manifest. As God says through Isaiah the prophet (Isaiah 58:6-9):

"This is the kind of fasting I want:
Free those who are wrongly imprisoned;
lighten the burden of those who work for you.
Let the oppressed go free,
and remove the chains that bind people.
Share your food with the hungry,

and give shelter to the homeless.
Give clothes to those who need them,
and do not hide from relatives who need your help.
Then your salvation will come like the dawn,
and your wounds will quickly heal.
Your godliness will lead you forward,
and the glory of the LORD will protect you from behind.
Then when you call, the LORD will answer.
'Yes, I am here,' he will quickly reply."

While there is therefore a cost to helping the needy, the orphan, the homeless, the naked, the prisoner and the hungry in practical ways, the spiritual benefits are huge. God's expansive heart is moved by these works. While works can never save a person on their own, when they are the expression of hearts that are compelled by the love of God to go to the least of these, then He sees this as the kind of worship – the kind of fasting, indeed – that He longs for and, in reward, He manifests His glory in revival power.

A Holistic Kingdom

Maybe you can see now why this third value is so important to us at Iris. Going to the poor leads us to embrace a three-dimensional kind of mission that we believe is true to the heart of Jesus Himself. In His first sermon, Jesus quoted Isaiah 61 as a full expression of what the Father had entrusted to Him:

"The Spirit of the LORD is upon me,
for he has anointed me to bring Good News to the poor.

He has sent me to proclaim that captives will be released,
that the blind will see,
that the oppressed will be set free,
and that the time of the LORD's favor has come."

Here we see all three components of mission: the saving (words, preaching Good News), the social (works, bringing freedom to captives and ushering in God's Jubilee), and the supernatural (wonders, the blind will see). Here almost more than anywhere else in Jesus' teaching we see the holistic nature of the Kingdom of heaven. This is the whole Gospel for the whole person throughout the whole world.

In 2010 I wrote about how revival fire was being powerfully sustained in Mieze. The Holy Spirit had first come years before, but the fire was blazing brighter than ever when we visited again. On that occasion we saw just how the presence of God's revival fire can be seen in beautifully kaleidoscopic ways. When the Holy Spirit moves in revival, and continues to move in sustained revival, we see people receiving more and more of Him on a regular basis. But there is no one way in which He moves and manifests. Sometimes we see Him when people hear the message of the Gospel and fall under heavy conviction; at other times in healing miracles; and at other times in building schools.

When I wrote up what I had witnessed, I pointed to what revival looked like. I wrote that, "In today's meetings it looks like deepest conviction; tears of desperation, repentance, longing and relief; quiet, glorious, weighty worship; and also the most energetic joy of the Lord…"

I then went on to add:

"The Presence in the bush of Africa also looks like homes, schools, farms, food, water wells, family, adoption of many children, fellowship, miracles, fun — the full spectrum of life in God!"

Going to the least of these and ministering the love of God to the poor in practical ways is all part of the three-dimensional mission of Jesus.

What it Looks Like

What does it look like to go to the least of these?

What does it cost us?

This is an important question because we need to combine romance with realism.

I will answer these questions with an account of our trip to Malawi in 2000:

"Malawi stretches ahead, its hills rising seven thousand feet below us from the Zambezi River valley of Mozambique. Pure, dazzling cumulus clouds add grandeur to the fresh, clear air of the north, far from the smoky brush fires that have polluted the skies of Maputo around our center in the south. Heidi and I are squeezed into our Cessna light plane, sharing precious space with everything we need for a crusade in the bush: sound system, generator, tents, sleeping bags, lights, tools, lots of water. With worship music on in our headsets, we prepare our hearts.

We are excited, studying the huts passing below us and praying to understand the needs of yet another country and mission field. A peak ahead blocks normal radio transmission to Blantyre, so we use short-wave to reach

Lilongwe and explain our intentions. What are we doing in Malawi? they want to know. We are holding a conference for almost one hundred of our churches in the unlikely town of Bangula in Malawi's southern tip, and we need to be there tonight.

I last visited Malawi in May, when we had eighteen churches that resulted from a two-day visit by our staff a year earlier. Now we have more than a hundred churches in this dusty, forgotten corner of the country where white missionaries are almost never seen. Thousands of believers are begging for this conference. They can hardly believe we will come this far to be with them. They are so excited. Many are walking for days from their villages to be with us. Even our leading pastors from Mozambique are enduring long, tortuous bus journeys over terrible roads to help us with this wildfire revival.

Fueled up at Blantyre, we head for Bangula, still sixty miles away. I know it only by its GPS coordinates. We drop over the hills down to a low plain, hot and shimmering in haze. I pick out rivers and landmarks I recognize from my chart. I hardly know what to expect. Silva, our lead pastor in Malawi, has been working for months getting the word out about these meetings. Is anyone coming? How will we take care of them?

Up comes a river that I know runs right by Bangula. A town materializes, but it is small and spread out. I see dirt roads and dry brush. And I see no runway where the map says it should be. I circle around.

'Help me look, Heidi,' I cry. 'I don't see any kind of airport!'

But there is a curious open field at the center of

town, crisscrossed by footpaths. Surely that's not the airfield? There are cows all over it and people wandering everywhere. Then I see the letters B-A-N-G-U-L-A dug in the dirt, obviously to be seen from the air, and a few markers at the corners of the field. A truck charges across the field, bouncing over the ruts through the crowds and I recognize it as one of ours, driven up days earlier from Mozambique.

I skim the ground to inspect the surface. There are holes, ditches and anthills, rocks and bushes, but I pick out a relatively safe line. Tanneken Fros, on our staff from Israel, is in the truck and waving energetically as we fly by her. This is the place. I go around. By now thousands of children are streaming across the field to watch us land. A few older guys are frantically waving them, and the cows, to the side with sticks. I coast in with full flaps and settle down as easily as possible on our oversize tires. The ground is rough and our plane shakes and vibrates to a stop in a cloud of dust. We are down and safe – and inundated with jumping, excited kids.

It's obvious that a plane hasn't landed here in years. This is an event! Everyone is staring. What have we brought? What is in that plane? We drag out our big speakers and heavy generator and are mobbed by helpers. Somehow everything gets loaded into the truck, we find guards for the plane, and we are off to our first meeting.

It's not in a church, or even a building. One of our Christians has a field with a couple of mud huts. We get there by driving in and out of deep gullies along a dry river bed, trying to remember how to get back.

There isn't much left of the town. Clearly the economy

is dead. The countryside is gripped by drought. Dust blows down the street in swirls. People sit in the shade and stare without energy. The few shops are almost bare. All is in disrepair. But we find our 'conference', a big band of ragged, dirt-poor country peasants who have been waiting for us all day. Tanneken has bought them sticks and plastic tarp, which they have put up between the huts for shelter. They even nailed together some rough boards for a speaker's platform, with its own roof of tarp.

It's windy. The tarps are flapping and dust is blowing everywhere. A couple thousand people are trying to find bits of shade. We set up the generator way off in the bushes where it won't be heard, position our big speakers, hook up our heavy amp, and we have a sound system! What a rarity.

This gathering is the poorest we have seen yet in Africa. All come without food. None of the children have shoes. Obviously most have never received medical care. There are swollen, infected eyes and feet, and terrible scabs and sores everywhere. To feed them we buy big cooking pots and all the beans and maize available in town. Our ladies stir these pots over wood fires through the day, babies strapped to their backs. Water is carried on heads from a well in a nearby village. We buy straw mats for everyone to lie on at night, and they sleep with their colorful skirts wrapped tightly around themselves. There are no lights apart from the flashlights we brought. We dig our own pit latrines.

But we came to preach, and we poured our hearts out for three days. Is everyone hungry for Jesus? Do we want His presence and touch? Do we want to be filled with the Holy

Spirit? Do we want to repent of all our evil and idolatry? Yes, yes, yes, yes!

What have we come here for? Nothing less than the love of God in Christ Jesus, who died for us! We'll never get love from a witch doctor. We'll never find enough in our families. We'll only find it in Jesus. If we have Him, we'll have everything!

We teach all we can from the Word of God in our short time together. The people flood forward in every meeting, kneeling in the dust and hot sun during the day and in the dark at night. They want everything they can get. There is no resistance to the Gospel. They know they are poor and helpless. This is their last chance, their only hope, and they know it. They are poor in spirit and theirs is the kingdom of heaven."

Chapter 4

Suffer For Him if Necessary

*"All praise to God, the Father of our Lord Jesus Christ. God
is our merciful Father and the source of all comfort. He
comforts us in all our troubles so that we can comfort
others. When they are troubled, we will be able to give
them the same comfort God has given us. For the more
we suffer for Christ, the more God will shower us with his
comfort through Christ. Even when we are weighed down
with troubles, it is for your comfort and salvation! For when
we ourselves are comforted, we will certainly comfort you.
Then you can patiently endure the same things we suffer.
We are confident that as you share in our sufferings, you
will also share in the comfort God gives us."*
(2 Corinthians 1:3-7)

At the gathering of Iris leaders in Pemba in July 2013, I said
the following about our fourth core value:

"We are willing to suffer for the sake of the Gospel. Suffering for the Gospel doesn't mean being unhappy. It actually can make you very, very happy because you're willing to show love to people out of love for God! You're willing to prove your love and by proving your love you will get a response from God. To the degree that we share in the sufferings of Christ, to the degree we are willing to show the world a love it has never seen before, we share in His reward and joy. We don't just pray for protection against anybody hurting us, or doing anything that bothers us. We learn the joy of loving no matter what anybody does to us or how they treat us. It's a joy to prove our love for God in this way! We're not stupid; we don't look for suffering. We don't try to suffer, but we're willing to suffer according to the will of God. The Bible tells us that He rewards those who suffer according to His will.

This is important to us as ministers and leaders. We do not love people or do them a favor by promising them God will protect them from all suffering. If He protected you from every chance to demonstrate the infinite, perfect, godly love that He has, He would rob you of your joy and your reward!

I've heard it said, 'We don't believe in the theology of Job anymore.' The New Testament tells us of the outcome of God's dealings with Job. Job suffered a lot and he didn't know when the suffering would end. But he never lost his faith. The result was that he lived hundreds of years longer, he was twice as prosperous as he was before, he had the most beautiful daughters in the land, and forever in heaven he will be glorified for being able to say, 'Though He slay me, yet will I trust Him!'

As leaders in Iris we need to have that same attitude.

I don't care how hard it gets. I don't care if God kills us – we're still going to trust our perfect Savior! I came to Mozambique ready to die right at the beginning. My life is gone. We're dead to the old life. Our lives do not belong to us. I don't want to take ownership of my life; I don't want to try to get God to give me everything I want in life. I want Him to change me! I want Him to give me His desires! I want His purity, His motives. That's what makes me relax! That's what makes me chill and just enjoy our God. I don't want prayer to be a constant struggle with God, trying to get Him to do something different than what He wants. Some people say, 'You know your prayer works if you can get God to change. I don't want God to change. He knows my desires better than I do. That doesn't mean I don't ask Him for things. I ask Him for all kinds of things. But I trust Him for what's perfect.

So, this is important, Iris leaders. We have to put up with whatever is necessary to fulfill God's purpose for our lives and get the best possible resurrection, to get the best possible reward, to get as close to God as we possibly can."

We Must Die to Live

We are often asked what the overcoming key to our ministry and growth is. We don't think in terms of keys or secrets, but of the simplest truths of the Gospel. We have learned by experience that there is no way forward when pressed to our extremities but to sacrifice ourselves at every turn for His sake, knowing nothing but Jesus and Him crucified.

We must die to live. It is better to give than to receive, and better to love than to be loved. We cannot lose because we have a perfect Savior who is able to finish what He began in us, if we do not give up and throw away our faith.

In years past we did not think we could identify with Paul like this, but now we understand more of what he meant when he wrote,

"We think you ought to know, dear brothers and sisters, about the trouble we went through in the province of Asia. We were crushed and overwhelmed beyond our ability to endure, and we thought we would never live through it. In fact, we expected to die. But as a result, we stopped relying on ourselves and learned to rely only on God, who raises the dead." (2 Corinthians 1:8–9)

Heidi and I get overwhelmed by our awareness that we are only jars of clay, very fragile and finite, capable of only giving out so much, and with very limited understanding and strength. But we have come to be encouraged by this very state of affairs, because God's power and glory will become obvious in our weakness. As Paul says in 2 Corinthians 4:7–10:

"We now have this light shining in our hearts, but we ourselves are like fragile clay jars containing this great treasure. This makes it clear that our great power is from God, not from ourselves. We are pressed on every side by troubles, but we are not crushed. We are perplexed, but not driven to despair. We are hunted down, but never aban-

doned by God. We get knocked down, but we are not de-
stroyed. Through suffering, our bodies continue to share in
the death of Jesus so that the life of Jesus may also be seen
in our bodies."

With All Perseverance

Many people today are running hard after a Christian walk
devoid of any suffering. They believe that they have a divine
right to healthy and wealthy lives, to a rich experience of
the power of God's glory without any hardships. This has
long been a problem for the Church throughout the ages.
It always boils down to this: some emphasize the Spirit but
neglect the Cross while others emphasize the Cross but
neglect the Spirit. The first, who promote a theology of
glory, say that by faith we can live free from any suffering,
confessing and possessing every miracle, naming and
claiming all kinds of material riches. The second, who
promote a theology of suffering, say that it is our constant
and inevitable lot as Christians to walk a life of pain without
breakthrough, because suffering is the crucible in which
God refines us.

Which one of these two positions is correct?

As so often, the truth does not lie at either end, but
in holding two kingdom principles in tension. These two
principles can be summed up in the teaching of Jesus. Here
are two extracts, the first to do with embracing suffering,
the second with miraculous breakthroughs:

"If any of you wants to be my follower, you must turn from
your selfish ways, take up your cross, and follow me. If you

try to hang on to your life, you will lose it. But if you give up your life for my sake and for the sake of the Good News, you will save it." (Mark 8:34-35)

"Have faith in God. I tell you the truth, you can say to this mountain, 'May you be lifted up and thrown into the sea,' and it will happen. But you must really believe it will happen and have no doubt in your heart. I tell you, you can pray for anything, and if you believe that you've received it, it will be yours." (Mark 11:23-24)

Here we see what it truly means to follow Jesus. Being a disciple means taking up one's cross and dying to self every day. It means being willing to give up everything for the cause of the Gospel. But this is not the end of the story. At every critical point in this self-forgetful life, the true disciple believes without doubting that nothing is impossible with God and that every mountain of difficulty will be cast into the sea. This includes poverty, sickness, death, spiritual darkness, persecution, and so on.

The true disciple lives a life of both perseverance and power. It is not either suffering or glory. It is both.

Paul once told the Corinthians, *"When I was with you, I certainly gave you proof that I am an apostle for I patiently did many signs and wonders and miracles among you"* (2 Corinthians 12:12). Notice the word "patiently". Other translations say perseverance. Paul was a man of both power and perseverance. He embraced both.

Our first several years in Mozambique were extraordinarily difficult. We had been partially prepared by our street ministries in Hong Kong and London, but our challenges in Africa reached the point of absurdity to the many people who could not comprehend our motivation for persevering. Then, through the years at many repeated points, just when we thought we had been through the worst testing, even greater faith challenges would confront us. Our life and ministry have been a course of ever-increasing faith as we have held onto our core values, which have always sustained us in the Lord. One of these has been "suffer for Him".

The Pain of Loss

What kinds of hardship have we been called to embrace for Him?

One of the hardest things has been when those we have loved have been called home to heaven. We have seen so much of this over the years, but one incident from March 14 1996 will have to suffice, concerning the death of a boy called Sumbane. This came as a result of him not being treated in time for malaria. At the time I wrote this:

"Sumbane died yesterday of malaria, even after a two-hour cold shower to reduce his fever. We had no medicine and couldn't get him to the hospital fast enough. Eight years old and one of our little orphans at Chihango, he knew Jesus and had been beautifully touched by the Spirit. Many prayers and tears flowed, but now he's in heaven where he can be so very happy. Our hearts are up there with him, where Jesus is. What a great day it will be when we and all the children of Chihango can join him and stand before our Lord without spot or wrinkle, full of joy and righteousness.

We have wept many tears over the years. But we have never grieved as those who have no hope. In every loss we have overflowed with the glorious hope of heaven, knowing that those whom we love and who have left us are in the presence of Jesus, who wipes away every tear from our eyes. In every loss we have not allowed our hearts to become bitter or our gaze downcast. Rather we have turned every defeat into breakthrough by contending for victories in the future in those very areas where we have witnessed momentary defeats in the past. In every situation of disappointment and loss, we have increased our perseverance and intensified our faith, knowing that what Paul says at the end of Romans 8 is true:

"Can anything ever separate us from Christ's love? Does it mean he no longer loves us if we have trouble or calamity, or are persecuted, or hungry, or destitute, or in danger, or threatened with death? (As the Scriptures say, 'For your sake we are killed every day; we are being slaughtered like sheep.') No, despite all these things, overwhelming victory is ours through Christ, who loved us."

Against All Odds

At times suffering for Him has meant continuing to believe that God will intervene in a situation when all the evidence suggests otherwise. These are times when we have been called to go on believing in the truths of the Gospel and the promises of Scripture even when it looks like breakthrough is the last thing that will happen.

When, in 2001, the terrible floods came to Mozambique there were outbreaks of cholera. This placed us right in the heart of one of the most intense battles we have faced. Here is what I wrote at the time:

"Challenges to our faith in Jesus do not stop. Last week, even as we received daily reports of desperation from the flooded north, a terrible outbreak of cholera hit our center at Zimpeto near the capital city of Maputo. We now think the cholera was introduced by contaminated food brought into a wedding in our church. The disease is wildly contagious and within days we had taken seventy children, pastors and workers to a special cholera hospital in town. This is actually a big tent, strictly quarantined, filled with cholera tables – bare wooden beds with a hole in each and buckets underneath for nonstop diarrhea and vomiting. Every patient was on an IV drip.

Many have died in this emergency hospital. Maputo's health officials were terrified of a citywide epidemic. Maputo's Director of Health put her finger in Heidi's face and told her, 'You will be responsible for killing half of Maputo!' Every day health officials came to our center, desperately trying to identify the source of the cholera and contain its spread. Soon the city police were involved, intent on shutting down our entire center and ministry. For days nothing seemed to help. We were washing and disinfecting everything. Our trucks were making hospital runs day and night. Our own clinic was filled with children on IVs. Our staff was completely exhausted.

Only Heidi was allowed to visit the tent hospital. Every day she would go in and spend hours and hours with our kids, holding them, soaking them in prayer, declaring that they would live and not die. They vomited on her, covered her with filth, and slowly grew weaker. Many were on the edge of death, their eyes sunken and rolling back. The doctors were shocked by her lack of concern for herself, and were certain she would die along with many of our children.

Our stress level was the highest ever. We remembered how we had been evicted from our first center in early 1997 and we just couldn't take that again. We had been preaching salvation and deliverance with all our hearts to these children we had rescued out of the streets and dump, and now they were slipping away right in front of us. Twenty of our pastors from the north were also in the tent and dying. Some of our weaker pastors desperately wanted to go home, certain that they would all die if they stayed with us. Heidi and I were ready, yet again, to quit if God did not do something.

But during all of this the Holy Spirit kept falling on our meetings. Again and again all visitors would come to Jesus and hungrily drink in His presence. A strong spirit of intercession came over our stronger pastors, who would pray all hours, not only for our cholera victims, but for the suffering of the whole nation. Intercessory prayer groups in the U.S. and Canada, and around the world, began to pray intensely for us.

Three days ago our entire future in Mozambique was in question. No one had any more answers. Our weakness was complete. Then some of our children began coming home from the hospital, even as others were being taken there. And then there were no more new cases. Then yesterday everyone was home! Just like that ... the cholera is gone. And Heidi is fine.

The doctors and nurses at the hospital are in a state of shock and wonder. The Director of Health again put a finger in Heidi's face.

'You! This is God! The only reason you got through this was God! You and dozens of these children should be dead!'

Eight of the medical staff there want to work with us now.

'This is miraculous!' they say. 'You know God! We've never seen God do anything like this. We've never seen such love! We don't want to work here anymore. We want to work with you!' And so they will.

Several visitors to our center who came down with cholera did die after returning to their huts and refusing to go to the hospital. And we heard that one of our pastors had died, but that report turned out to be mistaken. We did not lose a single person who lives with us at Zimpeto."

See how we cannot separate suffering from glory. So often we have been called to forget ourselves, expending every last bit of energy and love on those for whom there was seemingly no hope. In those times we have been stretched to our limits. Our faith has been tested to the utmost. But in the end the mountain has been cast into the sea and the reward of our believing, even when we've hung on by our fingernails, has been to see the miracle-working hand of God.

Fighting the Good Fight

Both Heidi and I have experienced life-threatening conditions, but we are not alone to face that among the worldwide leaders of Iris. It seems that many of us have had to pass through the shadowy valley of suffering and death from time to time. In 2002 I wrote:

"Surpresa Sithole, our Mozambican national director, seems incapable of a negative thought. Brimming over with the Holy Spirit, he grins broadly and laughs easily in all circumstances. He is my constant companion in the bush and we go everywhere preaching together. Jesus supernaturally called him away from his village, his witchdoctor parents, and has made him a powerful leader among our churches.

But for a moment today he is more serious. He is on the phone from South Africa and again we face a test of faith. Simon Ndubani, one of our strongest pastors and a member of our leadership commission in South Africa, is sick. Actually he is almost dead. Starting with coughing and diarrhea, he's been declining for a year but without money for a doctor has not been diagnosed. People suggest that he has advanced stomach cancer, or AIDS, but he's been tested HIV-negative. Normally a very big man, he is a shrunken shell of what he once was. In the last three days he has deteriorated precipitously. He is in great pain. He cannot eat. He cannot walk. Today he cannot even move or turn over in bed. His vision is blurry and in the last few hours he lost his speech and hearing.

It's hard to understand. Simon has been one of our most gifted preachers and has shown great faith. Jesus has used him to heal the blind and crippled instantly. Many desperate people in his church have come to him for prayer and have been delivered. He is known as a great man of God. But now he is at death's door, destitute and helpless. He has no money, insurance or health benefits. His family is without transportation. His wife is sobbing and at her end.

This is really terrible news. What of God's reputation? How will our churches handle such discouragement? What will we say? Surpresa and I pray over the phone, and we keep praying, along with many others. Surpresa drives Simon to a hospital and carries his thin, bony body to his room. Simon is in a coma and still Surpresa has to carry him to the toilet every ten minutes. It is such a mess. The doctor expects Simon to die tonight. If he lives three days, it will be a miracle. Simon's wife is so afraid and distraught she will not even come into the hospital to see him.

Surpresa, Heidi and I have major conference meetings coming up in a few days in Mozambique. We have to speak the Good News to thousands of sick and destitute people without any hope but Jesus. We cannot defend the Lord's reputation. We will just keep on loving Him. 'Simon is yours, Jesus. You be his God and doctor. We are yours, and we will keep living for you.'

And so through the night and the next day we keep praying for Simon and preparing for our meetings. Another night comes and Simon is still barely alive. On we go. There is no direction but up, into His heart. Saturday comes and

Surpresa is expected to open our regional conference for our southern provinces tonight. But he is still at the hospital with Simon. I call him again, fighting the good fight of faith, because he needs to drive right away to Mozambique.

Surpresa responds with majestic understatement. 'Well, it seems like a great miracle has taken place. I've been sitting here with Simon this morning and we've been talking and laughing for hours. In fact, Simon doesn't remember going to the hospital or even why he is here! He is fine. The doctors will give him some extra blood, do a few tests, and send him home.'

Surpresa leaves Simon money for food and transport and heads off to Maputo where we have a terrific meeting. Days later we hear by phone that Simon is one hundred percent fit and doing all that he used to do. Jesus has the last say!"

The Fear of Death

Toward the end of 2007 I began to face a very severe, oppressive attack on my health that lasted two years and took me to the brink of death with incurable dementia.

Heidi writes about the moment when, when all seemed lost, suffering perseverance eventually brought a glorious breakthrough:

"One day, while I was ministering in Pasadena, California, the doctor visited me in the hotel and said, 'You need to call your family and friends to come and say goodbye to your husband because in a few weeks he won't recognize them. He won't even be able to swallow and he will die.

This is incurable and although we believe in miracles, you need to understand the situation.'

The doctor took my daughter aside and said, 'Understand, your father is going to die. You need to go and see him.'

'Oh God, oh God, oh God,' we cried, but we were not afraid, because even death has no sting. The devil has been defeated and we are free from the fear of death.

The fear of death enslaves many hearts, but I am fearless and not afraid to die. I have been shot at five times, stoned, threatened with knives and machetes, slammed against walls and thrown in jail, and I tell you, beloved friends, I am a fearless little one. I am not afraid to die because I have seen the beauty of the realms of Jesus and I have proclaimed, 'Yes, Lord!'

When everything is shaking on one side and glorious on the other, what do you do, beloved of God?

What do you do when you see deaf ears hear, but still have a husband who cannot even put on his own flip-flops? What do you do?

Fix your eyes on Jesus; the apostle and high priest whom you confess is worthy of more glory than Moses.

One of the first people I called was one of our dearest friends, and Rolland's best friend, Mel Tari, a Christian leader who has walked with us for thirty-three years; in fact, he was best man at our wedding. Mel has seen and witnessed revival; he has seen the dead rise.

'I'm just not accepting that report. It just will not happen! I will not go and say goodbye to him. No way. No! Thank you very much. No!'

'Mel,' I said, 'I appreciate that, sweetie, I appreciate that, but we have prayed for two years. Everyone has prayed. You've prayed. You have raised the dead repeatedly, but this is what we are facing.'

'It is not God's plan. I am not facing it. I'm coming to get him and I'm taking him to Germany to a wellness center where they will pray for his healing while caring for his physical needs.'

'But Mel,' I replied, 'we have that here. Why do I need to drag him off somewhere else? We have had hundreds of people raised from the dead. He can't even travel.'

'I don't care. I'm coming to get him.'

As it happened a fellow who worked with us agreed to take him to Germany for health treatments where I would soon meet up with them. However, when I got there, Rolland was worse than before and I thought, *Now what will we do? Thirty people are flying to Mozambique to visit Rolland as the doctor suggested, but now they all have to change their tickets to Germany?* In my heart I thought, 'Lord, it just isn't fair. I don't think it's fair. I'm not liking this! What is going on?'

'I'm doing something,' the Lord replied.

'Please do it, just do it, God. I know that you are good. You are good all the time. I'm sure what you are doing is good, but I don't get it.'

After that I had to go back to Mozambique and leave Rolland under Mel's watchful eye in the wellness center. Our good friends, John and Carol Arnott, Georgian and Winnie Banov, DeAnne and Randy Clark, and many others counseled me to speak to his spirit.

'Speak to his spirit-man. Tell it to get up and wake up,'

they encouraged.

So, every day, I would call my husband and speak, 'Wake-up' into his soul. 'Wake up! Wake UP! Wake Up! Be alive! Fly! Restore! Think! Be free! Live! Love! Feel! Wake up, Rolland! It is time to awaken now! Wake up *now*!'

Within a few months we saw improvement as the Lord began restoring Rolland's mind, filling and occupying his house.

My sleeping man began to awaken, to remember, to care for himself, to walk, to call me!

Rolland used to fly bush planes for our ministry to help us reach more lost and broken for Christ. Guess what? He recently passed his flying exam!

Do you know what it takes to fly an aircraft? It takes a sound mind, coherency, and the ability to use complicated charts, graphs and instruments. God gave him back everything, plus, plus. God is giving back again! He is giving back what the enemy has stolen from you. Take it back, take it back! Step into a new place. Dance, rejoice, be free!"

Truly, God took us through a time of great suffering. We were forced to face head on the mysterious truth that the sick are healed and yet sometimes our very own are struck down. As Heidi put it so eloquently:

What do you do when you see deaf ears hear, but still have a husband who cannot even put on his own flip-flops? What do you do?

What you do is what Heidi and many others did: believe for the breakthrough with all perseverance, even when all seems lost.

In 2007-8 I went through my own crucifixion experience. But in what amounted to a resurrection, I was completely healed by God and restored to more fruitful ministry than ever. If we are going to see sustained revival, we are going to have to be prepared to suffer for Him.

Finishing the Race

Perhaps it is for this reason that our fourth value is so often regarded as controversial in many contexts in the West. To be a Christian in a Western nation is very different from being a Christian in Africa.

Can the Christianity of the West penetrate the far corners of even this incomprehensibly poor country?

Can our conferences and conventions back home, set in carpeted, air-conditioned churches, reach into the Mozambicans' world of dirt, rags, starvation, malaria and frequent death?

Can we, with our supermarkets and fast food, know what to say to a villager with only muddy water to drink and a handful of hard maize to feed his family for a week?

In our world we preach to people who can fly and drive to attend our seminars, eat at fine restaurants after our meetings, and sink safely into sheets and real beds in clean, dry hotels late at night when we are finished. In Mozambique we face people who struggle for hours and days through waist-deep mud to hear us, carrying their hungry, dying children on their backs and sleeping on the bare ground night after night.

As Westerners ourselves we have been forced to confront the greatest challenges, not least the challenge of seeing sustained revival in Africa as a continent. This is truly a great mountain. Surely it is too hard for the Lord? Surely this mountain will never be cast into the sea?

When times are very tough we can start asking serious questions about the possibility of a continent-wide revival. Why does our faith keep getting tested so? How much suffering and overwhelming need can there be in the world? How can the Church, even the Western Church, take care of it all?

In these times we make a choice not to quit but to keep on keeping on, believing that God will bring the victory. We decide that we will not shrink back. We set our hearts and minds on the things above not the terrible problems below. We have an infinite Savior and because He died for us, there will always be enough for those who receive His blood and flesh. He will glorify Himself in the world. He will do it in the darkest and most impossible of situations. We resolve to be carriers of His glory.

After all these years of preaching in the bush among the poor and faraway, we realize we have seen just the beginning of what God plans for Africa. North Africa, considered almost off-limits for the Christian gospel, is now beckoning.

Jesus has no competition once His reality, love and power are known. Angola and West Africa are calling. The multitudes want what is real. Our bodies are exhausted, our time is stretched beyond endurance, our wisdom for shepherding this movement is finite, but each morning we find ourselves renewed by the power of God. Our lives are worth nothing to us, if only we may finish the race and complete the task the Lord Jesus has given us – the task of testifying to the Gospel of God's grace (Acts 20:24).

Glory and Suffering

What strikes us most in our long history of ministry is that we as human beings invariably and drastically underestimate God and His power and glory. Our dim vision and remaining sinful nature still cause us to fall short of comprehending and apprehending God to the fullest extent possible. Jesus constantly proves Himself better than we think. As we continue to experience more of Him, we are astounded by our previous dullness and lack of faith. We daily, constantly repent of our past misjudgments. Our life-force consists of anticipating even more revelation of God's glory. We meditate continually on His greatness.

And so we learn that our ambition is to enter into that glory, to stay in heavenly places while in this life, to taste and drink of the nature of that glory, and experience the climax of that glory: ultimate relationship with the King! All power, understanding, authority and anointing flow from being connected and united with our all-glorious God.

Our fire and zeal derive from knowing there is no limit to the glory of God, and every day can be more extraordinarily glorious in Him than the previous.

We are also struck by the fundamental understanding that no power on earth can separate us from that glory. Our salvation is perfect and complete. Nothing can keep us from glorying in Christ Jesus to our hearts' content. It is that completely open door to perfect life in God that keeps us moving forward with unlimited motivation to preach the Good News to the poor.

The corollary to our apprehension of the glory of God is our knowledge of our own weaknesses. Our history in Iris has humbled and broken us to the uttermost. We have never been more conscious of our own weaknesses, inabilities and failures. Truly, we stay low and minister in fear and trembling. We have absolutely nothing to recommend ourselves in view of the surpassing glory of God. Our only possible response before Him is to go lower still, to die and become nothing so that He can become everything to us.

Our own pride and self-confidence are the biggest obstacles to our ministry, our greatest stumbling blocks, the most obvious chink in our armor. We find it so extremely relaxing and enjoyable to release all confidence in ourselves and simply glory in Christ Jesus. After we have done all, we throw our crowns down at His feet and take credit for nothing. The more we acknowledge our weaknesses and helplessness, the more the power of God rests on us.

Chapter 5

Rejoice in Him

"Let the godly rejoice.
Let them be glad in God's presence.
Let them be filled with joy.
Sing praises to God and to his name!
Sing loud praises to him who rides the clouds.
His name is the LORD —
rejoice in his presence!
Father to the fatherless, defender of widows—
this is God, whose dwelling is holy.
God places the lonely in families;
he sets the prisoners free and gives them joy.
But he makes the rebellious live in a sun-scorched land."
(Psalm 68:3-6)

In July 2013 I finished my overview of the five core values of Iris Ministries by talking about joy. You would think that after talking about suffering, as I did in the last chapter, joy would be the last thing we would value. But the truth is:

Suffering for the Gospel was never intended to be
a miserable experience, but rather one in which
indescribable joy and seasons of hardship
intertwine in a way that only God could imagine.

In the New Testament era, following Jesus cost believers everything. It brought them face to face with the Roman Empire where the Emperor was regarded as divine. He was worshipped as "lord", "savior" and "son of god" – the very titles that Christians reserved for Jesus and Him alone. As soon as a person came to a living faith in Jesus in that context, it brought them face to face with a system that claimed that Caesar was lord. Christians could not countenance saying that. For them, Jesus alone is Son of God, Savior and Lord.

Little wonder then that followers of Jesus were placed in the most extreme dilemmas. If they confessed Caesar as lord they would be allowed to live and to trade, enjoying all the benefits of being a citizen of the Empire. If they refused, confessing Jesus alone as Lord, then they would be severely punished – either exiled (like the Apostle John) or executed (like the Apostle Paul). The early followers of Jesus truly knew what it was to take up their cross daily. For some this meant being literally crucified at the hands of Roman authorities.

Yet, at the same time, the earliest Church, oppressed from all sides, overflowed in extreme joy. The Apostle Peter, who was eventually crucified upside down at the orders of the

Emperor Nero (so early Church tradition indicates), shared the Gospel boldly and throughout a region of the Roman Empire known as Asia Minor (modern Turkey). He became a spiritual father to a number of local churches in that area and wrote both the letters attributed to him in the New Testament to those hard pressed congregations. He tells these churches to rejoice in their sufferings. He says,

"Be truly glad. There is wonderful joy ahead, even though you must endure many trials for a little while." (1 Peter 1:6)

He then reassures them that this time of trial is for a season and that what the enemy intends for harm, the Lord will turn to good:

"These trials will show that your faith is genuine. It is being tested as fire tests and purifies gold – though your faith is far more precious than mere gold." (v7)

Finally, he reminds them that in the midst of suffering, they are filled with the fruit of the Spirit that is joy – an indescribably intense joy that is not just future but present:

"Though you do not see him now, you trust him; and you rejoice with a glorious, inexpressible joy." (v8)

Here we find the perfection of multiple perspectives: just as in the midst of great weakness, God's power shows up in marvelous ways, so in the midst of great suffering His joy grips us and overflows from our lips with unbridled laughter. Only the Holy Spirit could do that.

Back to Pemba

When I came to the last value, rejoicing in him, I said the following:

"This took me a lot to understand – years and years to understand. And I'm still learning more every day. And that is that life without joy is absolutely pointless! There's no point in giving God your life, serving Him, laying down, suffering and doing everything He says, if you don't enjoy Him! If at the end of the day you're not happy, then what's the point of everything? ... you need to get this! Paul says in Philippians – this is the Bible, remember; this is Scripture; this is a command; this is not a suggestion; this is so you can stay alive – *'Rejoice in the Lord, and again I say, rejoice!'*

Nehemiah says, *'The joy of the Lord is your strength!'* How many want twice the strength that you have? Then you're going to need twice as much joy! It's just that simple.

It was the persecuted Christians in China who taught me that joy is the energy of the Holy Spirit. Suffering Christians being persecuted are saying that *joy is the energy of the Holy Spirit!* So if you just walk out of here kind of bored, then I've completely failed tonight. All the other things I've said before (about finding God, being humble, going to the least and suffering for Him) are for your joy!

Jesus, the night before He died, told His disciples, 'I've told you all these things so that your joy might be complete.' Remember this when you're in Bible School. Remember it when you teach your people, when you preach in church on Sunday. You do all these things so that your joy may be complete! For the joy set before Him, Jesus endured the cross. It was His motivation for everything He did. You are going to need the same motivation.

This was hard for me to learn – that when you're down and unhappy and discouraged and you don't know what to do, when you have to force yourself through a day, when you're not happy and you're not full, that's not the reason you were made! If you're down and discouraged, you're not doing the will of God! You are not obeying God, you are not in His will, unless you are full of the Holy Spirit. Something needs to change. You need an infilling!

Joy was also the reward that the Father gave Jesus. God said, 'Because you loved righteousness and hated wickedness, I will anoint you with the oil of joy.'

How many want to be anointed with the oil of joy? I mean anointed as in drenched!

Some people think that this is not important, that it's only for a few. You may not like it, but you need it! You *need* it!

You need to laugh! We all need to laugh more tomorrow than we did today! It's your biggest weapon. Joy is your biggest weapon! If you can laugh when things get really, really tough, if you can laugh with the joy of the Lord, that's your weapon in the face of the devil!

I want everybody at Iris to have this weapon against the devil! Everybody at Iris needs to be given the power to laugh in the devil's face!

I have testimonies of when people faced sorrow and death, and God just told them to laugh. I'm saying, Iris family, that we desperately need to laugh – as well as cry, as well as everything else. I know we've shed a lot of tears, but that's not how we should end up. Every single day we shed tears, but I don't think that's how we should end every day. We need to laugh at the end of every day! Laugh really hard at the end of every day! That's God's gift to you!

I found out that Jesus is not only a teacher, a healer, a wise miracle worker and everything else, but he's also an entertainer. He's also very, very funny. He's very enjoyable to be around! The most fun thing in the world is to be a Christian. If it's not fun for you, try something else. God gives you more joy than any other god. I want Iris to be known for its joy! This is our direction, this is our core value. It's not optional!

We need God, we need miracles, we need to be humble, to go lower still and go to the poor but the Gospel also gives us joy as a reward, and at the end we are very, very, happy to have found our God!"

The Joy of Transformation

In the midst of all that we suffer for Him, Jesus keeps pouring out His joy into our hearts. This joy knows no limits. It bubbles up inside our spirits and then pours out of our mouths as we laugh, sing, praise and shout. We cannot stop ourselves. The limitless River of God flows like a torrent from the deepest recesses of our being, bringing us into the completeness of joy that Jesus promised and purposed. A joy that confounds the devil and astounds the world. As such our joy is both our greatest weapon and indeed a great witness. The devil hates it and the world marvels at it.

There are all sorts of occasions that have released His joy within us, resulting in scenes of relentless and unbridled rejoicing.

One of the greatest catalysts for rejoicing is when we see the transforming power of the Gospel at work within an individual or a community. Then, as we reap what we have sown, we enter into that harvest of joy that Jesus promised.

Let me share a few testimonies.

One time I wrote, "Chihango has changed. The orphaned and abandoned children here are continuing to taste the goodness and favor of their heavenly Father. It is pure joy to bring the comfort of God Himself to 'the least of these'. We have a clear vision for our children, who were once beaten, abused and starved, that God might,

'...bestow on them a crown of beauty instead of ashes, the oil of gladness instead of mourning, and a garment of praise instead of a spirit of despair. They will be called oaks of righteousness, a planting of the Lord for the display of his splendor.' (Isaiah 61:3)

When we see the transforming power of the Father's love in our children, we cannot stop ourselves from rejoicing. All the hardships endured in the season of sowing are forgotten in the ecstatic joy we experience in the season of reaping."

Sometimes we find that so many people have had their lives changed in a particular place we revisit that it's hard to find anyone who needs healing! So in January 2011 I wrote this:

"Many wanted healing prayer, so our team spread out and laid hands on the sick. The needs were relatively minor, as we've already been to this village so many times. It's hard to find blind and deaf people anymore around here, a real problem!

However, one man was healed completely who was hard of hearing in one ear, and totally deaf in the other.

In recent years we've seen a stream of people healed of deafness, nearly every week!"

It brings us great joy when so many have been visited by the healing power of God that we have to search high and low for anyone who needs prayer!

But it's not just physical healings that bring us joy. Deliverance miracles release the joy of the Lord as well. In June 2010 I wrote,

"We always pray for the sick at outreaches and usually significant miracles rivet everyone's attention. We did see physical healings, but tonight was unusual because the greatest need among the crowd was for deliverance from evil spirits and alcoholism. It is common here for demons to choke people by the throat in the night. Our team laid hands on everyone within reach. Relief and joy spread through the throng as the power of the Holy Spirit set one oppressed soul after another free. Jesus is the answer, always, for everything!"

Whenever we see the living Lord Jesus saving souls, healing bodies, delivering spirits, we rejoice because lives are being utterly transformed through the power of the Gospel.

The Joy of Graduation

When people are transformed to the extent that they go on to become disciples of Jesus, training in our schools, learning how to share the Gospel, going deep into the Word of God, we rejoice with inexpressible joy! Whenever we see people move up and on in God, it brings us great pleasure.

On the 2nd December 2009, I recorded:

"There is wild celebration, high energy African dancing, arm-in-arm! Hearts are bursting with praise! Many are hit by the intense power of the Holy Spirit and all the variety of His emotions! Singing with all their heart and soul! Faces dripping with perspiration, but full of joy! Missionaries praying for pastors; pastors praying for students; students praying for teachers; everyone praying for everyone!

This is graduation day for our Harvest mission school and Bible school. We are seeing a tremendous day of worship, blending black and white, rich and poor, foreigners and nationals as we mark the end of almost three months of classes and outreaches at our Pemba base.

Our speaker, Mel Tari, gave us a powerful message on the significance of this day in the plans of God for each pastor and student. We and the Body of Christ worldwide are winning the war against the powers of darkness and the African continent will not be left out!

It is exhilarating to watch our village pastors jump and shout as they sing, 'Go, go go!' They will go to the uttermost parts of this nation, carrying the Gospel with all the love and power they have been given. Pray with us for their safety, health, strength and anointing as they face every kind of challenge. Pray also for our mission students as they follow their calls throughout the world. Many are interviewing for long-term service with Iris and we are so blessed."

Immense joy results when people who were once lost, broken, oppressed and sick are saved, trained, commissioned and released to make disciples of all nations.

The Joy of Adoration

Even though we suffer for Him, following Jesus means inexpressible joy, especially when we worship Him. In the midst of great hardships, our times of worship are never joyless, despondent, low key events. They are full of joy — the *complete* joy that Jesus promised!

Here are some examples of joy breaking out even while we are hard pressed:

"We repaired Chihango's bakery and for several months were able to locate enough flour to bake bread for the children and almost pay for the flour by selling bread in local villages. But now an underground 'mafia' has hoarded all the flour in the city in order to double the price and we cannot bake bread any longer. And so, as I write, the children are down to meager rations and in danger of starving again.

The most important thing to know about Chihango is that in the middle of all their deprivation the children have joy, real and rich joy. This in turn brings joy to Heidi and me and keeps us going. You would be so encouraged if you could watch these children praying at length with all their hearts, exalting Jesus and resisting the devil. We wish you could hear them sing through the day. There is life and hope here and people are taking notice.

In this country it is our Chihango children who give us the most joy. They soak up the Holy Spirit like sponges and each day are worshipping and seeking the Lord more fervently. They march around singing and praising God even as they learn to clean up, pound nails, saw wood, paint walls. They fully expect God to provide for them and their future."

It is because we constantly see the life-changing power of God like this that the joy in our worship reaches levels of extraordinary intensity. Here's a report of the service one Easter Sunday:

"And so we began our Easter service. We sang fast, rhythmic African songs. We sang slow worshipful songs. We called out hungrily for the work of the Holy Spirit in our hearts. I preached an Easter message, emphasizing the unimaginably surprising and creative goodness of our God, our need to trust Him all the more through our troubles, and His desire to live among us as a foretaste of heaven. And then the children marched out singing across the grass and through the trees of Chihango over to our 'baptismal tank' – a small water cistern by our house.

For several hours we baptized children and also adults from our surrounding community. One-by-one they climbed into the tank, many grinning broadly. We questioned them closely concerning their commitment to Jesus and carefully recorded their names. A band of local Christians sang and danced beside us the whole time. Each child went down into the water in death and up again in resurrection life. They laughed with joy. We clapped and praised the Lord. We prayed and interceded for each one, that our children would become spiritual pillars, leaders and preachers and plain, humble servants of our King. Chihango never saw a day like this."

The Joy of Expectation

Is it easy to rejoice in every circumstance? I'm not saying it is always easy, but over the years we have learned from our countless breakthroughs that it only a matter of time before Jesus gives us the victory.

This faith, built on a foundation of innumerable testimonies of God's faithfulness, creates an expectation that releases joy in our hearts and from our lips. Whenever we are faced with a new test, we remember how steadfast God has been in our previous tests, some of which have been extreme. This gives us the ability to choose joy as we wait for the new breakthrough, knowing that God is going to give us yet another reason to laugh as we look and marvel at what He has done. As we await heaven's solutions to even the worst of our earthly problems, the anticipation of His in-breaking Kingdom fills us with inexpressible joy.

Here's an example.

"The mud from the rains has prevented sellers of firewood getting to the village markets, so we now have no wood to burn in our bakery oven at Chihango. The government has been supplying a pittance for food, but they've stopped even that, so now the children are depending on us for daily sustenance. We, of course, have no more resources in ourselves.

I was asked recently, 'How can you have joy in a situation like that?' I thought to myself,

'How can anyone have joy by looking in the other direction?'

We are actually filled with joy because the Holy Spirit has poured the love of God into our hearts and that is what it means to be alive. He will sustain us and the children because by His grace we are seeking first His Kingdom. As we have often said, we are not simply providing humanitarian aid. We are looking for the Kingdom of God among us and want nothing less than for Jesus to dwell among us and reveal Himself gloriously to the hurting and greatly disadvantaged."

Harvest Joy

Our foundational values at Iris mean that we are committed to finding God, being humble, going to the least, suffering for Him and rejoicing with inexpressible joy, even in the midst of hardship. These are the values that undergird who we are and what we do, and they are the values that we believe are essential for sustained revival in a community, city, country and even a continent.

In all this talk of our rejoicing, it is important to remember that the subject of our joy is Jesus. We rejoice IN HIM. We rejoice when we see how Jesus saves people, how He heals them of every kind of physical ailment, how He sets them free from spiritual oppression, how He liberates them from extreme injustice and gives them power when they were powerless and a voice where they were voiceless. These things bring us such extreme joy, not for their own sakes but because they are evidence of the supremacy of Jesus! When we see such unlikely transformations and such impossible graduations, we cannot stop laughing and singing. We truly rejoice IN HIM!

Whenever we see this kind of transformation, we enter into the joy of the harvest. Harvest time is when all the painful and arduous sowing turns to reaping. There is nothing quite like this. When sowing turns to reaping, we are always surprised by joy! But then Jesus promised that we would. In John 4:35-36, He said:

"You know the saying, 'Four months between planting and harvest.' But I say, wake up and look around. The fields are already ripe for harvest. The harvesters are paid good wages, and the fruit they harvest is people brought to eternal life. What joy awaits both the planter and the harvester alike!"

There truly is joy in the harvest.

Today, Mozambique, Africa and the world are filled with hungry, hurting people. They are lost. Their eyes are vacant and staring.

Do you see them?

Can you feel what Jesus feels?

Do you have His vision?

"The harvest is great, but the workers are few. So pray to the Lord who is in charge of the harvest; ask him to send more workers into his fields." (Luke 10:2)

Conclusion

Clarifying and communicating core values is a vital and indeed helpful exercise. In 2010 and 2013 we sought to bring greater definition to the things that we value in Iris. When we did, we reminded ourselves that we hold the following very dear in all that we are and do.

We value *finding God*. We long continuously to seek His presence. That is to say, we seek first His Kingdom and His righteousness, as Jesus commanded us to. We ache, pine and long for the manifest presence of God. We must have this or we die. It is the wellspring of life.

We value *depending on miracles*. In seeking more of God, we get lower and lower before Him, acknowledging time and again that it is not by our human might or strength that we receive the breakthrough but by His resources alone. Going lower and lower is an unavoidable pathway to sustained revival.

We value *going to the least*, to the poorest of the poor.

Going low doesn't just mean going low before God; it means going to the lost and the least, getting our hands dirty, doing whatever is necessary to give the poor the dignity and the opportunity that God wants for them.

We value *suffering for Jesus if necessary*. We do not separate the work of the Spirit from the work of the Cross, nor do we separate the power of His glory from the call to embrace suffering. For us hardship and heaven go together. This means that we have to go on taking up our crosses daily.

Finally, we hold dear the call to *rejoice in Jesus*. We have to recognize that the joy of the Lord is our strength and that when we are being refined like gold in the fire, this is the moment to give voice to that inexpressible joy that the devil hates. Rejoicing and revival go together!

Practical Values

It is so important, by way of conclusion, to understand that these core values are not conceived in isolation from the needs of the world. They are not the result of a working party locked in a room or a church board sitting in an office. These values have been forged on the anvil of real, hard, sacrificial and practical ministry. The research that led to the refinement of these values was accordingly never detached, cerebral, objective or scientific. Rather it was life lived in the presence of God and as such required art and emotion, description and feel, to articulate them. Every time we have fed a child, prayed for the sick, imparted the Spirit, trusted in the Lord, turned the other cheek, worshipped on our faces and rejoiced to be alive, we have put into action our core values.

These values are therefore not theoretical, abstract concepts to be taught in a college or a school, nor are they procedures, methods, courses, or programs to follow. They have to be caught. They have to be imparted miraculously.

Let me put it this way.

These values are an atmosphere, an attitude, a place, an energy, a flavor.

They are light and heat.

They thrill. They motivate. They direct.

They are spontaneous. They blend in perfection. They produce results. They create life. They minister. They bear fruit. They last.

They make the heart throb and swell. They dazzle. They are beyond comprehension. They amaze.

They are the Kingdom. They are the Scripture. They are the plain Gospel, once and for all delivered to the saints. They are the Good News of great joy proclaimed by the angels on the night of Jesus' birth. They are the hope of the world, without which ministry is crippled.

They are not new. They are not clever. They are not the invention and discovery of Iris Global. They are not unique to Iris. They are the inheritance of every believer.

They are under attack at every point by the enemy, but they are worth proclaiming and dying for.

Personal Values

The most important thing to realize then, is that these values are activated in relationship with a Person, and that Person is Jesus.

In fact, these values *are* Jesus!

It is one of the ironies of our religious mindset that in our zeal to be strategically biblical, we confine our rules of engagement in the ministry to the abstract.

We teach the knowledge of God, but do not know Him.

We set our minds and hearts on concepts, but do not experience them.

We teach love, but do not possess it.

We teach holiness, but do not know how to attain it.

We teach power, but it eludes us.

We teach effectiveness, but are not effective.

We teach principles, but they have no life.

We teach strategies, but they fail.

We teach technique, but are confused.

We succeed, but then are humbled.

We are trained and qualified, but are not equal to the task.

We are doctors of the church, but have lost our way.

We construct a religious world, but God is absent from it.

We reach the pinnacle of human achievement in ministry and are left with nothing.

If the core values of Iris are pursued abstractly, they profit nothing. Something absolutely mysterious must happen by the agency of God: they must become ours. We must experience them. They must be given to us. Ministry education is about learning to minister practically. But it is not like learning to be a doctor or an engineer.

It is God people need, not our expertise. It is love, peace and joy people need, not our sophisticated abstractions of these. We tell people what to do and how to be, but our instructions frustrate. We feed on abstractions, but starve.

We sign up for training, but are left empty. We set goals, but find nothing when they are met.

Our values need to become personal and they become personal in relationship with Jesus. We are nothing and have nothing unless we receive what is concrete and real from our personal relationship with Him. We are dead without His breath. Our education is nothing without Him.

We do not know how to impart our values, except to pray and ask. We can attempt to describe them, as I have here, but whether they take root and bear fruit is a function of God's agency. Our understanding begins with an awareness of our utter dependence on God in fear and trembling. We hold out empty hands in the desperate hope that He will share His nature with us. We take no credit even for our faith, or our choices.

By the grace of God we, the leadership of Iris Global, have core values that are personal and not abstract. Our values derive from a singularity, God Himself – a God who is not an impersonal unity, but a Trinitarian relationship. And our values are found only in relationship with Him. As he apprehends us, we starve for Him, we crave immediacy, we must know Him, we must find Him, we must live in Him, we must find all that we need in Him. We must be in love. We must be thrilled. We must be secure, romantically fulfilled and exploding with joy. We cannot leave Him for a second. We know how thoroughly frail our frame and constitution are, that we will die outside of Him.

Every desire of our heart is found only in Him. He is not an abstract belief, but our God whom we love.

Passionate Values

All this is to say that our core values are only discovered and activated in a passionate love affair with the living God. They are not the product of education or instruction. They are the result of the kind of revelation and wisdom that only comes from hearts that are beating to know God better and better. Everything that is productive in Iris flows from this place: the heart that is on fire with passionate love for God.

Our values are not the outcome of research;
they are the offspring of romance.

Productive ministry in the Kingdom of God is more than turning left or right as the Spirit gives us orders. It is more than teaching sound doctrine and laying hands on the sick. There is a missing ingredient that means everything to God. He simply wants to be loved! If He feels loved, if He is showered with our affection, there is nothing He will not do for us.

This love is not felt or expressed in striving. Straining to love Him with disciplined Bible study and controlled ministry programs, and even prescribed devotional techniques, is not love. The mystery of ministry is a contagious, imparted love born of God and in total freedom that makes all the difference. This love is found in rest, in relinquishing our own resources and abandoning ourselves in full surrender to the divine love. Only when that happens do we find what God values and the empowering love to see them earthed in practical ways. It is only when we choose being over doing that we find the lavish love of God.

"Do not awaken or arouse love until it so desires," says the Song of Songs. We fall in love with God as we fall under the Spirit's control. No one is blessed when their lover is straining to love them. God is not blessed by our strain. We should not be ministers and missionaries if we can possibly do anything else. He is the most jealous, emotional and romantic lover in the universe, and He knows if we are really loving Him in our ministries.

Nor does God feel loved if we do not enjoy Him, constantly and to overflowing. Our confidence in Him is reflected in our joy. We choose friends who enjoy us and in whose company we find joy. In ministry we are to be the friends of God, making Him feel loved and thrilled to have made us. In return we are filled and thrilled.

We are therefore not, in the first place, a ministry organization with job descriptions, strategies and goals. We do not "go to work every day and get things done". We are not an anthill, where each ant carries out its job precisely, carrying massive loads in absolute obedience, totally devoid of the emotion that we can carry in the Holy Spirit as creatures made in His image. We are a family filled with life and love. Relationships are all that matters.

Permeating Values
We take no credit for the ministry of Iris Global but recognize that each of these imparted values has affected, shaped and determined everything we have thought and done in Iris. Every one of them is brought to bear on each action we contemplate. We see them as obvious in Scripture. We

hardly recognized them as living, specific, discrete, non-optional components of our personal relationship with God until we reflected on what has characterized and propelled our ministry all these years.

Iris Global is not monolithic and pure through and through. Our values have not completely percolated among our widespread churches and ministries. But they have been the catalyst and made the critical difference. They are the "DNA" of Iris. They are the distillation of the whole council of God that we have received and our prayer is that they will permeate the life and work of Iris completely by the grace of God.

How then is this to happen? How are the values that are foundational to our ministry and critical to sustained revival to be imparted to others, permeating the whole of Iris? If educational programs, reliant on human wisdom and learning, are not the answer, then what is?

The answer is through the way we choose to disciple people in Iris. Whenever we turn our focus to making disciples, we reproduce in others the life and love that God has imparted to us. That means communicating the core values that have proved to not to be a passing fad, but a permanent foundation to all that we are and do.

How then do we replicate ourselves, disciple our people and train them for ministry? Of course, we provide all the education and skills we can, and impart all the gifts we can. But we will still totally miss the mark unless an indescribable mystery occurs: free, direct, spiritual, supernatural, mystical romance with God, and that without measure.

Our discipleship program consists of holding to our

core values, as described in this book. We are not allergic
to programs as long as they are not a substitute for the
presence of God. So of course we do have curricula, classes,
schedules, planned outreaches, small-group discipleship
gatherings, home groups, a unique Bible school format, a
missions school for foreigners and many other activities
that are the result of planning and preparation. But these
are channels and outlets. They are not the engine of our
ministry.

Whenever we see lives changed in our bush outreaches,
time is given to discipleship. I remember one time Heidi
sitting outside under a tree with the village's leading
Christians. They were, by now, her close friends. She taught
quietly and unhurriedly from the Scriptures. This is always
an extremely valuable time, the highlight of an outreach
in many ways. Earnestly and hungrily everyone was asking
questions and seeking all the more understanding. Our aim
is to *present everyone perfect in Christ* (Colossians 1:28).

The more we give ourselves to others, the more our core
values permeate the whole of Iris. This is done relationally
more than anything else and in that way these values are
caught more than taught.

Keeping the Fire Burning

The five core values that I have described in this book are,
I believe, a critical factor in sustaining revival over many
years in Africa. All this requires discipline. There are times
in every relationship where love can run dry. There are
times in every revival when the fire burns less intensely.
We can take our eyes off the object of our devotion. We can

forget the rock from which we were cut. We can become distracted by fads and lose focus on our foundations. Our first love can grow cold and the main thing can become the forgotten thing.

So when we have lost our motivation and are hearts run dry, we go back to what it is that we value most. When love starts to grow cold, we seek God's face. When we are in need, we trust in His supply. When we are at the end of ourselves, we go lower still and to the least of these. When faced with hardship and persecution, we choose not to lose our reward by retreating. And we resolve that our boundless joy will supply us with all the energy and direction we need.

Our course is to share with the world what we have received to the limit of the ability God gives us. This book is part of our legacy. May these five core values not only be taught but caught.

May a great fire be lit in your heart and in your ministry – a revival fire that will be sustained to the glory of God!

Epilogue

I return at the end to where I began: with the Person of Jesus.

Iris is not about us. It is about *Jesus*.

Revival is not about manifestations or miracles; it is about the Reviver, Jesus our Savior.

We only have one destination, one home, one reality, one resting place, one source, one motivation, one reward, one possession, one point of contact with God, one source of real satisfaction – and that is Jesus.

We cannot overemphasize Him in any way.

He is all we have and everything we need.

All we do is come to Him like children for everything.

His is the only name under heaven in which we trust.

He is our wisdom, sanctification and joy.

In Him we have no anxiety about anything. He provides our guidance. He is able to speak to us, to guide us, to thrill us by His Spirit. Our souls find our greatest delight in Him and He gives us the desires of our hearts.

Our five core values can be therefore condensed into one in Jesus we must enjoy life!

In Him we can laugh, for our worst trials and challenges are small in His sight. Our message is always Good News. We can only give Him praise and honor forever and ever.

The prophet Isaiah speaks of our Savior in Isaiah 25:4:

"You are a tower of refuge to the poor, O LORD, a tower of refuge to the needy in distress. You are a refuge from the storm and a shelter from the heat."

Everything we value has been found in Jesus. The key to our core values is therefore falling in love with Him.

Love is a gift of relationship, not just self-sacrifice. The secret place is not necessarily found in a prayer closet or a posture of soaking, or in battling for a just cause, or in a massive prayer and fasting effort. Even the most amazing miracles can leave us lonely and without relationship. We can run out of motivation advancing the noblest ideals and working at all levels to transform society. We can minister until we have no more strength, and still go home and lie in bed without the relationship for which our hearts are made.

Everything is okay with relationship. It is all that Jesus cares about, all that motivates Him. He could do many more amazing miracles and dazzle the world with His powers, but He is interested only in relationship. The entire creation, all the grandeur of the physical world, and all His works are designed to serve one thing: *relationship*. Revival has no content without it. Renewal and manifestations are pointless apart from it. Miracles only find their meaning in it. Joy is shallow and groundless unless rooted in it. Without relationship we are the living dead.

Let it then be shouted from the rooftops.

Iris is all about Jesus.

Revival is all about Jesus.

Without Him, there would be no core values.

But falling in love with Him over and over again we have discovered what matters most to Him and in the process have been given clarity about what we are to value.

As the Psalmist cries (73:25):

"Whom have I in heaven but you?"

About IRIS GLobal

Rolland and Heidi's roots

Heidi and I began Iris Global (previously Iris Ministries) in 1980, and have been missionaries since then. We were both ordained as ministers in 1985 after completing our BA and MA degrees at Vanguard University in southern California. I majored in Biblical Studies and Heidi in Church Leadership. I am a third-generation missionary born in China and raised in China, Hong Kong and Taiwan. I was greatly influenced by my grandfather, H. A. Baker, who wrote "Visions Beyond the Veil," an account of the extended visions of heaven and hell that children received in his remote orphanage in southwest China two generations ago.

"Blessed are the poor in spirit,
for theirs is the kingdom of heaven."
(Matthew 5:3)

Heidi was powerfully called to the mission field at age sixteen when she was living on an Indian reservation in Mississippi as an American Field Service student. Several months after she was led to Jesus by a Navajo evangelist, she was taken up in a vision for several hours and heard Jesus speak audibly to her and tell her to be a minister and a missionary to Asia, England and Africa. When she returned home to Laguna Beach, California, she began ministering at every opportunity and leading short-term missions teams. We met at a small charismatic church in Dana Point, and got married six months later after realizing we had the same radical desire to see revival among the poor and forgotten of the world.

Work in Asia and London

We spent our first six years together leading evangelistic dance-drama teams all over Asia, making use of our backgrounds in creative media and the performing arts. But we increasingly came into intimate contact with the desperately poor, and could no longer be satisfied by large meetings and quick visits to various locations, even though thousands were coming to Jesus. We had to learn to come to a stop and take care of long-term needs, one person at a time.

We began by working with the poor in the slums of central Jakarta, Indonesia, and then among the forgotten street-sleepers and elderly in the most crowded urban area in the world, central Kowloon in Hong Kong. Jackie Pullinger's work among drug addicts in the Walled City was a major influence in our lives.

In 1992 we left Asia to do our PhDs in systematic theology at King's College, University of London. But we couldn't stop ministering to the poor, and so at the same time we planted a warm and thriving church community for the homeless of downtown London, joined by a kaleidescope of students, lawyers, businesspeople and friends from many countries. We learned the composite beauty of the Body of Christ!

Mozambique

For years we longed to get to Africa in fulfillment of our calling to prove the Gospel in the most challenging situation we could find. We wanted to see a continuation of "Visions Beyond the Veil" and believed with my grandfather that the most likely place to see such revival again was among the most unlikely! So we were drawn to Mozambique, officially listed at the time as the poorest country in the world.

A few days into my initial visit to Maputo, Mozambique's capital, I was offered an orphanage that no one could or would support, not even large churches in South Africa or European donor nations. It was horribly neglected and dilapidated, with eighty miserable, demon-afflicted orphans in rags. I thought it was a perfect test of the Sermon on the Mount. Our Father in heaven knows what we need. Seek first His Kingdom and righteousness, and these things will be ours as well ... Take no thought for tomorrow. Why worry? Jesus is enough for us, for anyone.

Alone and without support, Heidi and I offered to take over the center and provide for the children in return for the opportunity to bring the Gospel to them. Within months the children were saved and filled with the Holy Spirit, weeping while still in rags with gratitude for their salvation. Jesus provided miraculously, more all the time as our children prayed night and day for their daily food. We brought in teams, improved the center, and took our children to the streets to testify to more orphaned and abandoned children. Some were lost in visions, taken to heaven and dancing around the throne of God on the shoulders of angels.

But abruptly, after we got up to 320 children, the government evicted us and denied our children permission to pray and worship on our property. Totally without a back-up plan, our children marched off the property barefoot without a home. We lost everything. We also lost tremendous amounts of support because we welcomed the increasing presence of the Holy Spirit in our meetings.

But we were only beginning to taste the power of God in Mozambique. Land was donated by a nearby city. We got tents and food from South Africa. Provision came in from supernaturally touched hearts all over the world. Soon we could actually build our own dorms. Bush pastors longed for a Bible school, and to receive what our children had received from the Holy Spirit. Graduates went out and began healing the sick and raising the dead. Church growth in the bush exploded.

Then revival was fueled exponentially by the desperation caused by catastrophic flooding in 2000 when three cyclones came together and brought torrential rain for forty days and nights. More damage was caused by that flood than Mozambique's many years of civil war. A cry for God rose up like we had never experienced or imagined, and our churches across the country multiplied into thousands. God provided a bush airplane, which we used constantly to spread the Gospel through remote "bush conferences" at dirt airstrips in every province.

Expansion in Mozambique

There are networks of churches and church-based orphan care in all ten provinces in Mozambique in addition to bases in main cities. In recent years we have personally concentrated on the Makua, a people group in the north who were listed by missiologists as nearly unreached. With tremendous help from missionaries and nationals, since 2002, over two thousand churches have been planted among these people.

Each year thousand of visitors come to help us at our various bases, and we have a missions school in Pemba that offers something special to us: missions training on the mission field! Here we combine teaching, worship and spiritual impartation with everyday application to ministry among children and the poorest of the poor, both in towns and in the remote villages of the African bush.

IRIS Global

Iris has over 35 bases in about 20 nations led by teams of missionaries and local leaders. As more and more people want to associate with us spiritually and in every way possible, our Iris family is expanding country by country, a step at a time. Bases are being established, works are being initiated, and in developed nations fervent believers wanting to participate with us in the Gospel are starting Iris charities. We welcome short-term and long-term applicants, and stress that Iris is a holistic ministry not limited to particular specialties. It includes evangelism, Bible schools, medical clinics, primary and secondary schools, farming, vocational training, church planting, bush conferences, counseling, child sponsorship and in the future, a university in Pemba for the poor! We make ourselves available to the Holy Spirit to make use of every gifting He brings our way. We celebrate the life of God among us in all its variety!

We are deeply encouraged by the fervent interest in ministry to the poor that we have encountered all over the world. We would like all those who want to work with us in some way to familarize themselves with our history, teaching and core values. A good place to start is our first book, "There is Always Enough," detailing much of the story of how we got to this point. Another must on my short list is my grandfather's book, "Visions Beyond the Veil".

In summary, we value immediate intimacy with Jesus, a life of utterly-needed miracles, concentration on the humble and lowly, willingness to suffer for love's sake, and the unquenchable joy of the Lord, which is our energy, motivation, weapon and reward – not optional!